VOLUME 6

SCORE!

FOR ONE-ON-ONE TRAINING

Super Closers, Openers, Revisiters, Energizers

BY

Becky Pike Pluth, M.Ed., CSP

Rich Meiss, MBA

Karen Carlson

Scott Enebo, M.A.

Janice Horne

Doug McCallum, M.Ed.

Marc Ratcliffe, M.Ed.

Adrianne Roggenbuck, M.Ed.

Priscilla Shumway, M.Ed.

Enhanced Results for One-on-One Training

SCORE! FOR ONE-ON-ONE TRAINING:
SUPER CLOSERS, OPENERS, REVISITERS, ENERGIZERS, VOLUME 6

By

Becky Pike Pluth, M.Ed., CSP
Rich Meiss, MBA
Karen Carlson
Scott Enebo, M.A.
Janice Horne
Doug McCallum, M.Ed.
Marc Ratcliffe, M.Ed.
Adrianne Roggenbuck, M.Ed.
Priscilla Shumway, M.Ed.

Cover design by Studio810 (formerly Majeres Graphic Design)
Internal layout by Alan Pranke
Compiled and edited by Rich Meiss
Copy editing and proof reading by Liz Wheeler

ISBN: 978-0-9794103-4-5

10 9 8 7 6 5 4 3 2 1
Printed in the United States of America

Publisher
Creative Training Productions LLC
14530 Martin Drive
Eden Prairie, MN 55344

For additional books or quantity discounts, contact:
The Bob Pike Group
Phone: 800-383-9210 and 952-829-1954
Fax: 952-829-0260
Email: csheffield@bobpikegroup.com

THANK YOU TO MENTORS, COLLEAGUES AND CLIENTS

We thank our many mentors, colleagues and clients with whom we've had the privilege of working throughout our careers in the training and human resource development field. You have sharpened our minds and helped us develop many of the concepts which we now teach.

Thank you to the tens of thousands of presenters, trainers and facilitators with whom we've worked over more than 30 years. Many of you have given us great ideas, and/or allowed us to try out these ideas in your sessions. We appreciate the chance to work with so many great people.

We extend a special thank you to all the training consultants of The Bob Pike Group. Karen, Scott, Janice, Doug, Marc, Adrianne, Priscilla, and Michelle—you bring a professionalism and passion to your training that makes it a joy to work together. Thank you for your commitment to participant-centered training and for your creativity in putting together so many exercises like these.

Thank you to Jody Clark, Alan Pranke and Liz Wheeler for your graphic design and editing skills.

And a special thanks to the loves of our lives, Brad Pluth and Barbara Meiss, for your encouragement and continued support of projects like these.

Becky Pike Pluth and Rich Meiss

I'd like to extend a very special thank you to Rich Meiss for creating the SCORE! brand with our dear friend Doug McCallum and for his tireless work on this project.

Becky Pike Pluth

CONTENTS

INTRODUCTION

Training One-on-One Has Unique Challenges!

Many organizations find it necessary to train one-on-one or one-on-few, yet most trainers struggle with how to perform this task successfully.

Trainers who have embraced the techniques of The Bob Pike Group's Participant-Centered training approach may find themselves at a loss when it comes to training one person or just a few people at a time. The concept of breaking larger groups into four-to-six participants working together in table groups no longer applies, and many of the activities and exercises that work for groups of more than 10 are no longer possible to use.

In situations where an employee needs training immediately, one-on-one training needs to be done, but many trainers find themselves going back to the lecture and PowerPoint approach knowing it is probably not going to get the best results but unsure of what else to do.

This compilation of Super Openers, Closers, Revisiters and Energizers is the answer to this dilemma.

SCORE! for One-on-One Training provides participant-centered trainers with over 50 ideas to revitalize their training in these individual situations. The techniques, tips and activities listed here have been tested in the crucible of real training situations and proven successful by Bob Pike Group trainers. And a bonus is that many of these exercises will also work well for groups of a larger size!

Spice up your one-on-one or one-to-few training with applicable openers and closers. Revisit your content in new and fresh ways. Stimulate and engage your participant with fast energizers. This SCORE! book is organized to help you quickly determine an activity or exercise that will work for you and your participant(s). Choose from these four categories:

Closers—to help tie things together and end a session with impact;
Openers—to help begin a session in a powerful way and draw your participant into the content;
Revisiters—to reinforce key learning content in fresh and engaging ways; and
Energizers—to keep your participant mentally stimulated and physically activated throughout.

This is not a novel to be read straight through from start to finish. Use the Table of Contents to help you choose what activities are most relevant to your material or pique your interest. Training one-on-one can provide great opportunities to enrich your life and the life of your trainee in ways very few, if any, other methods of training can. Use these activities to springboard your content, your participant's recall and the enjoyment you both receive from the interaction. Let training be fun again, and stop dreading the one-on-one!

Becky Pike Pluth, M.Ed., CSP, MPCT
President and CEO, The Bob Pike Group

HOW TO USE THIS BOOK

Here are four simple steps for using this book effectively:

1. Remind yourself why it is important to use closers, openers, revisiters and energizers—even when training one-on-one—by reading the first page of each chapter.
2. Select the appropriate category—closers, openers, revisiters or energizers.
3. Pick the best exercise for your content and purpose.
4. Practice, practice, and practice the exercise before you actually use it.

Why use Closers, Openers, Revisiters and Energizers?

Each chapter gives more detail about the reasons to use these CORE exercises in your presentations, but here is a general overview.

Too many presentations simply start and end without a process or purpose. Yet research reveals that people remember best what they see or hear first and last, so we need to start strong and end strong—using good openers and closers. The purpose of revisiters is to make sure the participants really learn the content. A favorite phrase we use is "just because you said it doesn't mean they learned it." Revisit content multiple times with a variety of methods to ensure learning takes place. And energizers are used to keep participants alive in the session.

What Categories Are Included in the Book?

Although many of these exercises can be used for multiple purposes, we have divided them into four key categories, with energizers having two subcategories:

Closers | **O**peners | **R**evisiters | **E**nergizers

They are the CORE to help you SCORE and win in your training sessions. Each exercise has been placed into one of these categories and put in that section of the book. In addition, we have often indicated that the exercise may be used for another purpose. For example, several of the revisiter techniques are also good energizers.

How Do I Decide Which Exercise to Use?

There are many details to consider before choosing an exercise. What is my purpose? What do I know about my audience, and will this exercise work for them? What about time and space considerations? What materials do I need, and how much will it cost to purchase them? Will participants be able to gain a learning point and apply it as a result of the exercise? You can answer these questions briefly by glancing at the format of each page.

Why Do I Need to Practice the Exercise?

Good presenters make an exercise look easy, but usually that is only because they have used it a number of times. Our experience is that we need to try out an exercise several times—either on some friends and relatives in a low-risk setting or in front of a mirror by ourselves—before we have the word track and the flow down to use it effectively. Remember the six Ps: Proper Preparation and Practice Prevent Poor Performance!

Enjoy these CORE exercises!

SCORE FOR ONE-ON-ONE TRAINING—SUPER CLOSERS, OPENERS, REVISITERS AND ENERGIZERS

CLOSERS

The most important training "real estate" is the beginning and ending of your session because this information is what gets remembered the most easily! It's the rule of primacy and recency. So when you're training, don't use your closing as a way to promote the evaluation form, or worse yet, just end! Close your session with impact and purpose, even if you are just working with an individual or a small group. Make sure that you have a closing ACT.

A closing ACT includes **A**ction planning, **C**elebration, and **T**ying things together.

Action planning gives a participant time to reflect on the important concepts or ideas learned in the session and create a plan on how he or she will use the information back on the job. Multiple studies have shown that when people commit to making changes, they are much more likely to follow through. And when people plan the logistics of how and when they will make those changes, the probability increases even more. Use your closing time to help your learner achieve this!

Celebration gives participants who have invested time, energy and perhaps even money a chance to relish the new insights and skills they have gained as a result of the training. During your time together, your learner may have made difficult decisions, solved tough problems, or provided valuable input. All of these are reasons to celebrate his or her investment and revel in these accomplishments!

Celebration can take many forms. It might be something formal, such as a certificate of completion given at the end of the training, or it might be an informal celebration with the awarding of a small prize or gift card, or congratulations from the boss.

Tie things together when you close. A great presentation comes full circle. Training sessions circle back to the stated objectives to make sure participants are satisfied with the outcomes. An opening exercise that is used is referred to again as the program is concluded. Then close with a powerful ending—a quote, story, question, or call to action.

Here are some great, proven training closers for you to use in your one-on-one sessions.

AROUND THE WORLD IN 60 SECONDS ☐ ☐ ☐

Author : Janice Horne

Description: Participants close their eyes and take a trip around the world in 1 minute. Then they close their eyes again and take 1 minute to visualize what they want to accomplish (completing a project from beginning to end, steps they will take with their new learning, etc.)

Objective: To encourage a participant(s) to quiet his or her mind and visualize completion of an action as if it were already finished

Audience: Any training audience

Time: 5–10 minutes

Group Size: Any size, and great for one-to-one or one-to-few

Materials: Paper and a writing instrument

Process: Ask your participant to close his eyes and take a trip around the world in 60 seconds. Tell him you will watch the time. After you say go, have complete silence in the room. After 1 minute, invite him to open his eyes, and ask him if he made it around the world. He will nod yes. Then inform him that he will be applying the same process to: a project, an upcoming presentation, an action he will take back on the job, etc. (use whatever you want to reinforce and have him act upon from the training). You will once again invite him to close his eyes for 1 minute in total silence. Call time after 1 minute.

Debrief: Have your participant take additional time to write down some ideas he got from his minute of silence and then share it with you or one other person if there are others in the training.

Variations: The "around the world in a minute" portion of this activity could be used as an opener. The second part of the activity could be used as the closer.

CHEAT SHEETS ☐ ☐ ☐

Author : Scott Enebo

Description: Do you remember the sigh of relief when your teacher would tell you that you could take a "cheat sheet" to the test? Do you also remember, after hours of making this cheat sheet in tiny writing, not needing it? We know that content we learn can be hard to recall later. One key mechanism to recall is writing (not typing) things down. This activity is aimed at getting learners to recall what has been taught and lock it into long-term memory for use later.

Objective: To write down key learning ideas on an index card or a sheet of paper to better aid retention on any key concepts covered

Audience: Any training audience

Time: 5-60 minutes

Group Size: One-on-one or one-to-few

Materials: Index card or sheet of paper

Process:

1. Say, "You have the next ___ [instructor sets the time limit] minutes to look through all of your materials and make a cheat sheet on an index card that captures key concepts that you would want or need access to during a test on this content. This should be organized in a way that makes sense for you and is easy to access."
2. Allow time to create.
3. Give a test or else quiz the learner on key topics to see if she has mastered the content.

Debrief: This activity does not require a debrief as it is positioned as a content revisit.

Variations:

1. Reverse roles and allow the learner to quiz you as the instructor about concepts that are written down on the index card. If you get the answer correct, then you get to ask a question in return.
2. If working with multiple learners, have each person look at someone else's cheat sheet and see what is missing and what could be added.

DECK IT TO YOU ☐ ☐ ☐

Author: Doug McCallum

Description: This closer asks the participant to play a simple card game like Go Fish, Slap Jack, Spades or Hearts.

Objective: To check comprehension and revisit jargon and definitions critical to the training content in a fun and quick way

Audience: Participants in any training that has multiple terms, jargon, etc., related to the training

Time: 1–5 minutes

Group Size: One-on-one or one-to-few

Materials: One deck of playing cards [whichever game the trainer deems appropriate to the content] per person with terminology from the course/training written on each card in the deck with a black permanent ink pen.

Process:

1. Play the specific card game according to the rules.
2. Stop when you think you have a winning hand. The participant can only win by defining the terminology on the back of each card in the winning hand. If the learner cannot do that, the game continues.
3. Play as many games as you would like in the time allowed!

Debrief: When the game is over, those cards that couldn't be accurately defined need to be discussed until the definition is clear and agreed on by all parties.

Variations:

1. Change the card game.
2. Change the decks.

DON'T BLOW IT! ☐ ☐ ☐

Author: Adrianne Roggenbuck

Description: A participant blows up and ties off a balloon then tries to change its shape without breaking it.

Objective: To manipulate the filled balloon without breaking it and see how the learner's efforts to change the balloon correspond to efforts to implement a new skill

Audience: Any training audience that is learning a new skill

Time: 10 minutes

Group Size: One-on-one or one-to-few

Materials: One deflated balloon per person

Process:

1. Instruct the participant to blow up the balloon about ¾ full, leaving plenty of room to tie it off.
2. Ask the participant how she might be able to change the balloon's shape now that it is inflated. She might give you answers like: break it, squeeze it, push on it, etc.
3. Tell her to change the shape of her balloon without breaking it.
4. Have her show you how the shape has changed and tell you what she did to make that happen.
5. Now have her write the new skill she wants to implement on the balloon with a fine-point permanent marker and tell you what steps she will take to begin the implementation.
6. Ask her to change the shape once again as you begin the debrief.

Debrief: When you are attempting to implement a new skill, or make a change in your behavior, it is like trying to change the shape of your balloon. It takes constant pressure. What happens when you take pressure off the balloon? It goes back to its original shape. This is what happens when you stop applying the new skill consistently and you fall back into your old habits.

Variations: This activity could also be applied to organizational change as it takes constant pressure to keep the change initiative going. As soon as the pressure is released, the balloon goes back to its original shape, as does an organization when the change initiative is not consistently implemented.

FOLD YOUR HANDS ☐ ☐ ☐

Author: Rich Meiss

Description: Have your participant fold his hands the opposite way he usually does. If he usually has his right thumb on top, have him now make sure his hands are folded with his left thumb on top.

Objective: To show participants how difficult it is to change the way we do things

Audience: Any training audience

Time: 3 minutes

Group Size: Any size, including one-on-one or one-to-few

Materials: No materials necessary

Process:

1. Ask your participant how long he thinks it takes to change a habit. After he responds with a guess, share that research today indicates it takes an average of 66 days of conscious practice to change well-established habits.

2. Then ask him to fold his hands. Ask if his left or right thumb is on top. Then ask him to fold his hands again, but this time put the fingers together so that the opposite thumb is on top. Ask him how this feels. He may reply that it feels weird, unnatural, or strange. Tell him that this is what doing something differently feels like and that it will take a long time for this new behavior to feel natural.

3. Explain that this same principle will be true as he tries to implement the new skills and behaviors he has been learning in class. Because the behavior is new, it will feel strange or weird for some time as he practices it.

4. Tell the participant that he needs to find ways to reinforce his new learning and behavior in order to change it to permanent status. Otherwise he will tend to go back to doing things the way they've always been done.

Debrief: Discuss ways your participant can reinforce the new behavior back on the job and who he can count on as supporters to help him practice and stick with the new behavior.

Variations: Have your participant fold his arms, noting which arm is on top and which hand is tucked in. Then have him reverse his arms so that the opposite arm is on top and the opposite hand is tucked under. This will also feel weird and makes the same point.

NOW YOU'VE DONE IT! ☐ ☐ ☐

Author: Adrianne Roggenbuck

Description: A participant will close her eyes and visualize herself being successful using the new skills she has learned. She will then describe what that looked and felt like.

Objective: To help the participant visualize being successful using the new knowledge and skills she has gained in the training

Audience: Any audience involved in skills training

Time: 5-10 minutes

Group Size: One-on-one or one-to-few

Materials: None

Process:

1. Instruct the participant to close her eyes and take a deep breath.
2. Now have her visualize herself back on the job implementing the new skills she has learned. Have her imagine in detail how she would be using these new skills successfully.
3. Let her open her eyes and think about what her vision looked like and how it made her feel now that she has "done it."
4. Have her verbalize her feelings.

Debrief: Visualizing the utilization of new skills is another form of practice. Your brain will remember the visualization as strongly as a memory of a real event, so it is important to visualize doing the skill correctly. Also, the brain wants to repeat pleasurable experiences, so if the person felt good during the visualization, she will have a higher desire to repeat the action that gave her pleasure.

Variations: Have the participant sketch or write out her responses.

POSTCARD TO A FRIEND ☐ ☐ ☐

Author: Marc Ratcliffe

Description: Ask your participant to consider one or two key things that he would like to implement after the program based on what he has learned. This may include something he should start doing or perhaps something he should stop doing. He then will mail this to an "accountable" friend who will hold him to his goals.

Objective: To identify key items to put into practice post-training and someone to hold him accountable for that

Audience: Any training audience

Time: 10 minutes

Group Size: Any size, including one-on-one or one-to-few

Materials: Postcards, writing instruments

Process: Provide your participant with a blank postcard and ask him to write one or two things he would like to implement post-training. These points should be written on the back of the postcard. Next, ask him to address the card to a friend (or self-address the postcard if he prefers). Finally, collect the postcard, attach stamps and mail it on the participant's behalf about 3 weeks after the training.

Debrief: "Postcard to a Friend" acts as both a closer to content as well as a reminder of the content post-training. There will be greater impact for the participant as he is essentially creating advice for himself from himself with the twist being a friend will hold him accountable. The arrival of the postcard can also kick-start the implementation process, if it hasn't already started. Encourage the participant to contact his friend after a month to discuss the information on the card.

Variations:

1. The trainer could take a photo of the participant earlier in the program and create an actual postcard using his photo. This will make the feedback more personal and will encourage the recipient to keep the postcard for ongoing review and reflection.

2. If there is more than one participant, you could have them send postcards to each other. In this way, they could be the "accountable people" for each other. This variation would be particularly useful if the trainer was using a learning partner or study buddy throughout the training process.

☐ ☐ ☐ RADIO SCRIPT

Author: Marc Ratcliffe

Description: The participant is given a formula to create a radio script for news stories. This activity supports cognitive processes as it requires the participant to review material from the session and find key sound bites or newsworthy content.

Objective: To reinforce key content in a fun way through the creation of a mock radio script

Audience: Any training audience

Time: 30-45 minutes

Group Size: Any size audience, including one-on-one or one-to-few

Materials: Access to course reference material, writing instrument, paper

Process: Introduce the activity by explaining that the participant will be identifying key messages from the session's content and then creating a script for a series of short news stories. The trainer should provide her with "Tips for Writing Radio News" on the following page and provide examples of how the stories could be written. Once the news stories are completed, the participant should share them with you. This will provide some light-hearted reinforcement of the key material. In a larger audience, these stories could be recorded and rebroadcast to the rest of the group.

Debrief: The trainer should provide feedback on both the subject matter and the technique of the radio script. Where appropriate, feedback could be sought from peers also.

Variations: Although it is intended that these radio scripts are to be presented live to the trainer or a small group, they could be recorded and transformed into a podcast. This option would be particularly appropriate for online learners.

Tips for Writing Radio News

Anchor Intros

The place to start is usually the "anchor intro." This is what the announcer will say to introduce the story. An anchor intro quickly sets up your story and puts it into context. If it is the first story, it should also introduce the newsreader.

e.g. "Welcome to learning news of the day, I'm Rich Cake. Scientists in Finland have proven that smiling improves health...."

Telling a Story

All good stories have a clear start, middle and end. As you write your narration, try to tell a story which draws listeners in by setting a scene, raising a question or introducing a character.

e.g. "Environmental protesters are blockading a big XYZ petrol station in Houston. They say they're angry about the impact of the oil giant's work on the environment and also the way they believe it treats people in developing countries. This comes a week out from a crucial XYZ board vote on expanding operations in South America."

Adding Sound Bites

To extend the story, a short sound bite of an expert third party may be appropriate. This could be a statement from a roving reporter, a witness at the scene or an authority on the subject.

e.g. "In breaking news, creative training techniques improve retention by up to 90 percent. Bob Pike Group President Becky Pluth explains...."

Length

These stories should be a maximum of three or four sentences or 50–70 words long.

SEEDS & WEEDS ☐ ☐ ☐

Author: Janice Horne

Description: The participant writes down new ideas, skills, or tasks he has learned (seeds). Then he writes down what he will need to do to nurture those seeds to grow (pull weeds).

Objective: To encourage the participant to plan for application of his new learning while considering the obstacles he may face and how he will overcome those obstacles

Audience: Any training audience

Time: 5 minutes

Group Size: Any size audience, including one-on-one or one-to-few

Materials: 3x5 card or piece of paper

Process: Ask your participant to visualize planting a flower or vegetable garden. What seeds would he plant? Invite him to take a 3x5 card and write "Seeds" on one side and "Weeds" on the other. On the side of the card that says "Seeds," have him list all his new learnings and how he plans to apply what he has learned. On the side of the card that says "Weeds," have him list those obstacles that could keep his seeds from producing and what he can do to remove those obstacles.

Debrief: Your participant shares the information on the card with his trainer. With a larger group, have the participants share with a learning partner.

Variations: This activity could be expanded to include a metaphor with the whole planting and growing process: Seed, Soil, Sunshine, Rain, Weeding, Harvest.

THEN AND NOW ☐ ☐ ☐

Author: Karen Carlson

Description: The participant creates a list of new knowledge she has acquired since going through the training and celebrates it.

Objective: To assist a participant in recognizing and celebrating what she has learned during class

Audience: Any training audience

Time: 3–5 minutes

Group Size: One-on-one or one-to-few

Materials: None, although balloons, small prizes, gifts or certificates would be nice

Process: Allow the participant a few minutes to review her notes and create a list of things she now knows that she did not know at the start of class. Ask her to stand up and share her list while pausing between items for celebration—thumbs up, golf clap, whoop, etc. If you have more than one participant, have them take turns sharing one item from their lists at a time.

Debrief: Congratulate your participant on all she has learned and encourage her to continue learning.

Variations: The participant's list could be shared with her manager as a teachback or review opportunity.

THREE IN 3 ☐ ☐ ☐

Author: Becky Pluth

Description: The participant brainstorms training concepts covered and then selects her favorite three concepts to which she adds her own thoughts and prior learnings. She then shares these with the instructor who may record them.

Objective: To drill down on the core aspects of what has been covered with efficiency. This allows the instructor to know to what degree the learner has mastered the topic.

Audience: Any

Time: 5–10 minutes

Group Size: One-on-one or one-to-few

Materials: Video recorder (could be a cell phone with enough storage for a 3-minute video)

Process:

1. Instruct the participant she will have 2 minutes to brainstorm the concepts that have been covered up until this point and summarize the key ideas, key messages, concepts, or data points she has learned.

2. After time is up, give her 2 more minutes to select her top three ideas and add her own thoughts, prior learning and connections to those concepts to add value. This provides an opportunity for your learner to link her learning. Consider a starter question to help the participant launch into ideas like: What link can be made? What does this remind you of? What could you add from your experience?

3. The final phase is sharing. Your learner will have 3 minutes to share her three ideas. I recommend recording these and saving them for future one-on-one examples. Let her know how much time she has left by showing three fingers, then two and finally only one finger means her time is almost up.

Debrief: Watch the video and ask the learner what her takeaways are. Debrief by filling in any gaps she may have in her knowledge to ensure accuracy.

Variations: This activity could also be applied to larger groups but done in pairs and shared back in table groups. So one pair would share with another pair from a different table. No video recording would be done in this instance.

THOUGHT BUBBLES ☐ ☐ ☐

Author: Scott Enebo

Description: There are key ideas that come up during training that can capture the essence of what was taught as well as ideas to share with future learners. We don't always know what learners are thinking about, though, so it can be helpful to find ways to extract this wisdom and have it shared. Enter "Thought Bubbles!" Think about transforming learner thoughts and insights about the training into thought bubbles just like in the comics!

Objective: To share the best wisdom and insights from the training for others to hear and see

Audience: Any training audience

Time: 5–10 minutes

Group Size: One-on-one or one-to-few

Materials: Large chart paper cut into "thought bubbles"

Process:

1. Say, "In front of you, there is a thought bubble that would appear over your head as if you were in the comics. As you think about what you have learned or talked about today, what would you put in this bubble to help others better understand the value and impact of this information and how it can help you in your work? Take the next 3 minutes to write down this key insight on the thought bubble."
2. Allow time to write.
3. Have the learner post the learning on the wall for others to see and then share it with you, the instructor.

Debrief: The act of sharing ideas fulfills the criteria for a closer, so no debrief is required.

Variations: If this exercise has been done with enough people and you have posted the ideas on the walls, instead of having each learner write something new, have each learner look at what has been written and:

- choose a key idea and stand by that idea,
- share the significance and impact of that learning, and
- explain how the learner might use it on-the-job moving forward.

SCORE FOR ONE-ON-ONE TRAINING—SUPER CLOSERS, OPENERS, REVISITERS AND ENERGIZERS

Openers

People remember what they hear first and last the best. So start your training sessions with a bang and not a lot of housekeeping details especially if you are training one-on-one!

An opener is an activity that gets people thinking about the content and meeting you and other learners, if they are present. We use the acronym BAR to help you easily remember the intent of a good opener. Does it **B**reak preoccupation? Does it **A**llow networking? Does it **R**elate to content?

Break preoccupation. Participants come to meetings, presentations and learning events with all kinds of distractions, such as business phone calls to be made, deadlines to be met, or the fight with the kids that morning over unfinished homework. For this reason, a good presenter recognizes that he must break through this preoccupation barrier, because it can be the biggest enemy to capturing the full attention of the participants. The key to breaking preoccupation is involvement. Participants can ignore the presenter when training is done in a larger group, but it is much more difficult to ignore you, the trainer, when you are actively interacting with the learner and working to accomplish a task together.

Allow networking. Adults usually come to learning events with some experience in the topic. The good presenter will want to tap into that experience throughout the presentation or training. To accommodate this, she will work to get herself and the participant acquainted and comfortable with each other. Then, throughout the session, she and the learner or learners will share ideas and experiences with each other, thus enhancing the learning for all. Most adults don't want to attend a "sit and get" event; they want to take part, think, contribute and learn.

Networking also reduces tension. Participants come into a learning environment wondering, "Can I contribute? Will anything make me look or feel foolish?" The faster the learner gets comfortable, the faster he or she will be open to learning.

Relate to the topic. Most participants want practical take-away value. To demonstrate this value right from the start, the strong presenter will begin with an opener that relates to the content. Poor presenters often start with a story or a joke that might be funny but has nothing to do with the content or the event. Make sure your opener has a connection to the topic at hand.

Break preoccupation, Allow networking, and Relate to the content. By following these three suggestions, you will find that your opening will raise the **BAR** of your presentation, meeting or training event. Following are some time-tested one-on-one training openers that meet these criteria.

BEE-HIVING

Author: Doug McCallum

Description: The participant places hexagon Post-Its® on a flip chart in a random but systematic fashion.

Objective: To capture brainstormed ideas and create new, workable solutions for a certain task or topic

Audience: Any training that is focused on accomplishing a task or solving a problem

Time: 10–15 minutes

Group Size: One-on-one or one-to-few

Materials: Two different colored pads of hexagon Post-Its per person, flip chart paper, and tape

Process:

1. Ask the participant to write a problem to be solved on one color Post-It and place it in the middle of a piece of flip chart paper.
2. Then instruct the participant to take a set of Post-Its of another color and write down anything that comes to mind when thinking of this problem, one thought per Post-It. Do this for approximately 5 minutes.
3. Tell him to look at all the ideas he has written down and start hooking or grouping them around the original Post-It stating the problem. One side of the hexagon will hook to another side and so on. When this process is done, you will have a beehive of ideas.
4. Have him step back and see if there are any correlations that can be made. Are there any Post-Its that can be linked in another way? What great ideas surfaced because of the bee-hiving effect?

Debrief: When you are attempting to brainstorm, tools such as bee-hiving will help you discover good ideas, or ideas that work. That's the goal.

Variations: This activity could be applied to larger groups as well but each person or group of two should have their own board with their own Post-Its. Then have each group compare and contrast and pull off the best ideas from both and combine.

COMMON GROUND

Author: Karen Carlson

Description: The trainer and participant trade a few questions as they work to discover common ground.

Objective: To find commonalities shared by the participant and the trainer. This will also identify differences.

Audience: Any training audience

Time: 3–5 minutes

Group Size: One-on-one or one-to-few

Materials: None

Process: The trainer and participant take turns asking questions or making statements to determine if they have common ground in that area or not. The trainer will go first to model expectations. Questions might start with "Do you like...?" Statements could begin with "I don't like...." Examples might be "Do you like chocolate?" or "I don't like horror movies." Initial questions should be general information, without getting too personal. After a few questions about each other, add some that relate to the content of the class or the company.

Debrief: Make the point that we can likely find common ground with any other person if we get to know them well enough. Also make the point that differences or unique qualities in people make life interesting and allow us to learn and grow. Discuss with the participant how these commonalities and differences might enhance the learning process.

Variations: None

DISCOVERING LEARNING PREFERENCE

Author: Rich Meiss

Description: Ask your learner a few pointed questions to gauge her preferences for learning.

Objective: To discover the learning preference of the participant and therefore target the instruction to make the learning more effective

Audience: Any training audience

Time: 5–7 minutes

Group Size: One-on-one or one-to-few

Materials: A formal learning style instrument, if desired. Otherwise, no materials needed.

Process: In our Train-the-Trainer Boot Camps at The Bob Pike Group, we utilize a formal learning instrument called the Personal Learning Insights Profile. This self-assessment instrument measures the learning preference of the participant along three continuums—what is the learner's **purpose** (to be informed or to learn something practical), what is the learner's learning **structure** (does she want general or very detailed information?) and the **activity level** the learner employs when solidifying the learning (Does she want to reflect quietly on the content? Does she want to participate with others while assimilating the information?).

An alternate way of discovering this about the learner is to simply ask a few questions about his or her learning preferences. Some examples of this include:

Ask these questions, to which **Informative Learners** would generally answer yes:

- Do you like to learn for learning's sake?
- When you surf the web, do you find yourself going from one site to another to check out more and more information?

Ask these questions, to which **Practical Learners** would generally answer yes:

- Do you like to learn mainly when you are going to use the information?
- When you go to the web, do you find the information you need and then go back to what you were doing beforehand?

To gear your teaching style toward these learners, give informative learners a lot of additional "nice to know" information, such as extra examples or more reading material. Give practical learners just the "need to know" information that will help them learn the specific content you are teaching.

Ask these questions, to which **Specific Learners** would often answer yes:

- When you open a present or toy that needs to be put together, do you read all the instructions before you begin?
- When you cook or bake something, do you follow the recipe carefully?

Ask these questions, to which **General Learners** would often answer yes:

- When you open a present or a toy that needs to be put together, do you begin to assemble it and only read the instructions if you are challenged?
- When you cook or bake something, do you tend to do it from scratch?

To gear your teaching style toward these learners, create a lot of structure for specific learners. Let them know your agenda and objectives, give them specific time frames for the class, and give them a sense of the flow of information and exercises. Give general learners a global overview of what you will be covering, but allow them the opportunity to structure the information in a way that works for them.

Ask these questions, to which **Reflective Learners** would generally answer yes:

- Do you enjoy learning by yourself?
- Do you like to read or work on the computer to discover information for yourself?

Ask these questions, to which **Participative Learners** would generally answer yes:

- Do you enjoy learning with others?
- Do you like to have group discussions or exercises as a part of your learning?

To gear your teaching style toward these learners, allow reflective learners to study and learn on their own when appropriate. Let them read and reflect on the material, and then answer questions they might have. With participative learners, have a lot of discussions and activities to keep them engaged.

Debrief: While this information is primarily for the benefit of the instructor, you may find it useful to debrief with the participant at the end of a module by asking how your instruction met her need and if there is anything she would like you to do differently as you train her.

Variations: Use any variety of formal learning style assessments that are available in the marketplace, provided they are valid and reliable. Use the next page to mark the learner's preferences along the continuum and remind yourself of the type of instruction that will be most favored by him or her.

DISCOVERING LEARNING PREFERENCE

Continued

LEARNING PREFERENCES CONTINUUM

Name of Participant: ______________________________

Informative Learner ←→ **Practical Learner**

Give informative learners a lot of additional "nice to know" information, such as extra examples or more reading material.

Give practical learners just the "need to know" information that will help them learn the specific content you are teaching.

Specific Learner ←→ **General Learner**

Create a lot of structure for specific learners. Let them know your agenda and objectives, give them specific time frames for the class, and give them a sense of the flow of information and exercises.

Give general learners a global overview of what you will be covering, but allow them the opportunity to structure the information in such a way that works for them.

Reflective Learner ←→ **Participative Learner**

Allow reflective learners time to study and learn on their own when appropriate. Let them read and reflect on the material, and then you can answer questions they might have.

With participative learners, have a lot of discussions and activities to keep them engaged.

EFFECTIVENESS GRID ASSESSMENT

Author: Rich Meiss

Description: Have the learner go through the assessment grid. This can also be used as a pre- and post test on the content to check for knowledge growth and comprehension.

Objective: To allow the participant to assess his knowledge and skills in the content of the program

Audience: Any training audience

Time: 15 minutes

Group Size: Any size group, and excellent for one-on-one or one-to-few training

Materials: Copy of assessment grid and a writing instrument

Process:

1. Ask the participant to make a list of the characteristics of a good _____________. In our coaching program, for example, we ask them to think of a good coach or mentor in his or her life and list all the attributes that made that person a good coach. If you have several participants, combine their characteristics on a chart.

2. Show the participant your pre-developed assessment grid which lists the key attributes you have pre-determined. These characteristics should also be the knowledge and skills that you'll be teaching in the class. Make sure to leave 3–5 blanks so that the participant can fill in several of the attributes she has listed. (See sample grid on the next page.)

3. Ask the participant to rate herself on a scale of 1-10 (or 1-100). The low number means she has no knowledge or skill in that area, and the high number would mean she is a complete master in that area. Ask her to rate herself honestly. On the blank lines, she may add several of the characteristics she came up with.

4. After rating herself on the scale, ask her to list at the bottom of the page her three greatest limitations (lowest scores) and her three greatest strengths (highest scores). Discuss the results with the participant or have her share several of her strengths and several of her limitations with a learning partner.

Debrief: Tell the participant that these are the areas the training will address, and encourage her to build on her strengths and upgrade her limitations.

Variations: None

COACHING EFFECTIVENESS GRID

Look through the list of characteristics mentioned below. Next, ask yourself, "How effective am I as a Coach?" and rate yourself on the scale from 1 to 10. 1 is low effectiveness (no skill), and 10 is high effectiveness (a complete master).

	1	2	3	4	5	6	7	8	9	10
1. Identify what "good" looks like and what the goal is (expectations)										
2. Communicate those expectations										
3. Observe performance (inspect gaps)										
4. Cheerlead good performance										
5. Redirect poor performance										
6. Ask good questions										
7. Listen effectively										
8. Provide balanced feedback										
9. Encourage to be the best										
10. Adapt to personal needs										
11. ______________________										
12. ______________________										
13. ______________________										

Three Coaching Limitations

1. ______________________
2. ______________________
3. ______________________

Three Coaching Strengths

1. ______________________
2. ______________________
3. ______________________

GETTING TO KNOW YOU, GETTING TO KNOW ALL ABOUT YOU

Author: Priscilla Shumway

Description: The instructor and learner take turns answering questions about their work experiences that help them get acquainted.

Objective: To create a fun and stress free way to become acquainted with the new learner. New learners are often worried about whether they will be successful at the job. They may question whether they have the knowledge or skills to succeed or, during training, if the instructor will be helpful and open to their needs. It is important to start the session by creating a fun and stress free way to minimize their concerns and create an open learning environment.

Audience: Any training audience

Time: 5 minutes

Group Size: One-on-one or one-to-few

Materials: Question cards

Process: Create a series of question cards as shown below, or create your own. The learner can select a card at random and answer the card. The instructor then selects a card at random. You might start each session with a few of these questions to further the relationship and get better acquainted.

- What is an accomplishment from your prior job that you are proud of?
- Share an embarrassing story from any former employment.
- What is a job related nightmare that you have had in the past?
- Who was a mentor or coach (teacher, instructor) who was helpful in your past?
- What are you most excited about/worried about with this new job? (New hire)
- Where do you see yourself in 5 years?
- When someone asks you what you do for work, what is your "elevator speech"?
- If you were going to post a tweet on Twitter about this job, what would you say?
- What social networks do you use? How do you use them?

Debrief: None

Variations: The questions for additional sessions could be tailored to revisiting what was covered in prior sessions.

☐ ☐ ☐ GINGERBREAD MAN

Author: Marc Ratcliffe

Description: The participant will identify strengths and weaknesses pertaining to the training topic on a sheet of paper with an image that loosely looks like a gingerbread man.

Objective: To create a visual representation of strengths and weaknesses of the learner regarding the training content. By acknowledging where she is now, as well as where she wants to be, the participant can begin to take steps to develop herself to fulfill her goals. It also means the trainer has a visual clue of where the participant believes she is at and where opportunities for growth may exist.

Audience: Any training audience

Time: 10 minutes

Group Size: One-on-one or one-to-few

Materials: Blank Gingerbread Man template (see example), different colored pens

Process:

1. Provide the participant with a copy of the Blank Gingerbread Man template. Explain that she is going to build a picture of herself using the image on the sheet. First she is going to identify her strengths. Cognitive or knowledge-based strengths could be linked to the head, psychomotor or tactile strengths could be linked to the hands or legs, and affective or emotional strengths could be linked to the main body.

2. Once the strengths are completed, ask the participant to identify weaknesses in much the same way. However, this time she should use a different color, so it is easy to distinguish between strengths and weaknesses. Provide her with an example to support her own development. (A completed template example is available after the blank template.)

This is a useful opener as it establishes a literal picture of where your participant is and what gaps she presently has. This will provide important insights for both the trainer and participant alike. In addition, participants are often more likely to provide an honest assessment of themselves when transferring to an inanimate object (like a gingerbread man) rather than speaking about themselves in front of others.

Debrief: Given the personal nature of the activity, it is important for the trainer to be sensitive to the participant responses. If you are doing this in a group, thank them all for their contributions, and explain that there are no wrong answers and that this activity will help them to identify gaps in their knowledge and skill which the following training will address.

As new knowledge and skills are acquired through the training, participants should be encouraged to return to their Gingerbread Man to add or remove items as necessary. This can be a very motivating action towards the conclusion of their learning process.

Variations:

1. For the artistically inclined, physical features, color and clothing could be added to the picture to add vibrancy.
2. As an extension, the trainer could ask the participants to do a before and after version of their gingerbread man using two different templates. The "before" shot would represent where they are now and the "after" shot would represent where they hope to be at the end of training.

GINGERBREAD MAN

GINGERBREAD MAN – COMPLETED EXAMPLE

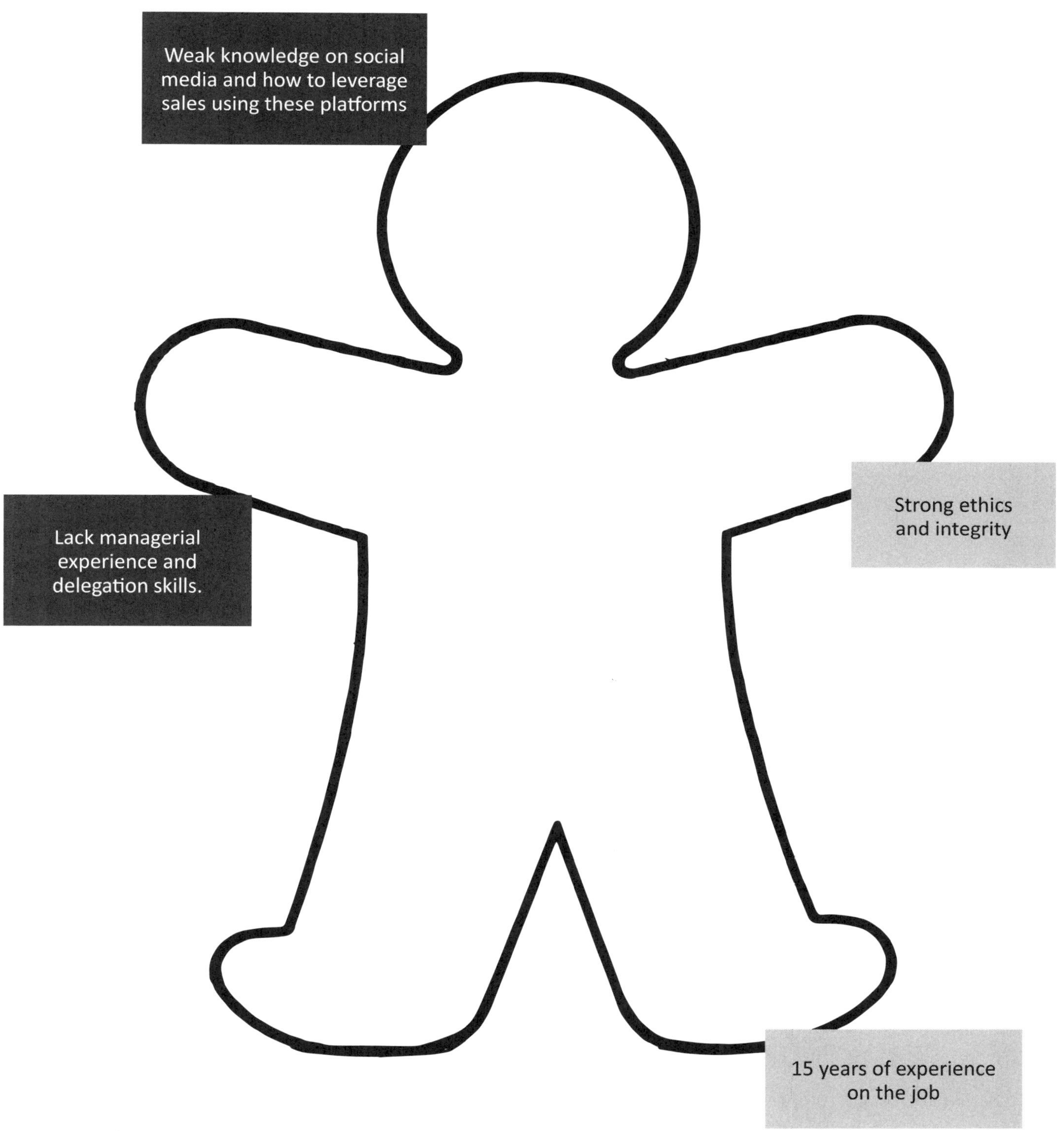

HOME BASE

Author: Marc Ratcliffe

Description: Home base is both a goal-setting and reflection exercise which helps to focus participants on the personal outcomes desired for the training. It is a document that they return to many times during the training and could be used at both the start of the day to orient the participants and at the end of the day to reflect upon the journey. In this way, they will always return to their "home base" to check to see if they got what they needed from the training and to devise plans to move closer to their goals.

Objective: To write key personal goals to achieve from the training and create a mechanism to reflect upon those goals

Audience: Any training audience

Time: Initially, 10-15 minutes, then ongoing reflection throughout

Group Size: Any size, including one-on-one or one-to-few

Materials: Poster paper, writing instruments

Process: Give the participant the Home Base template (see example on the following page). Explain to him that he is going to participate in a personal goal setting exercise and that these goals relate to what he wants to achieve as a result of the training. The goals are broken up into three sections:

- **Core Goals:** These are the non-negotiable things that he wants to be able to achieve by the end of the training. These should be written in the smaller circle in the middle of the sheet.
- **Extended Goals:** These are extra things that are "nice to have" by the end of the training. These should be written in the medium-circle.
- **BHAGs:** Researcher and author Jim Collins talks about BHAGs, or "Big Hairy Audacious Goals." Challenge the participant to come up with a few amazing goals that could be achieved with some work as a result of the training. Although they may seem crazy, it is important to dream big. Ultimately, while these may not be achieved during the training, they could provide the impetus to create some further development post-training. These goals should be written in the outer or largest circle.

Once complete, the participant is to write his name at the top and either post on the wall or some other prominent place. If training is being conducted mainly on-the-job, the home base sheet could be posted at his workstation.

Debrief: At different stages during the session, the participant should be encouraged to return to his "home-base" and reflect upon his progress. He should highlight or check off any goals that have been achieved or add additional ones based on exposure to new content.

Variations: Where there is more than one participant, "home base" can be transformed into a group goal-setting exercise. This would be particularly useful if there was a specific organizational need that was common to each participant.

HOME BASE

Name:____

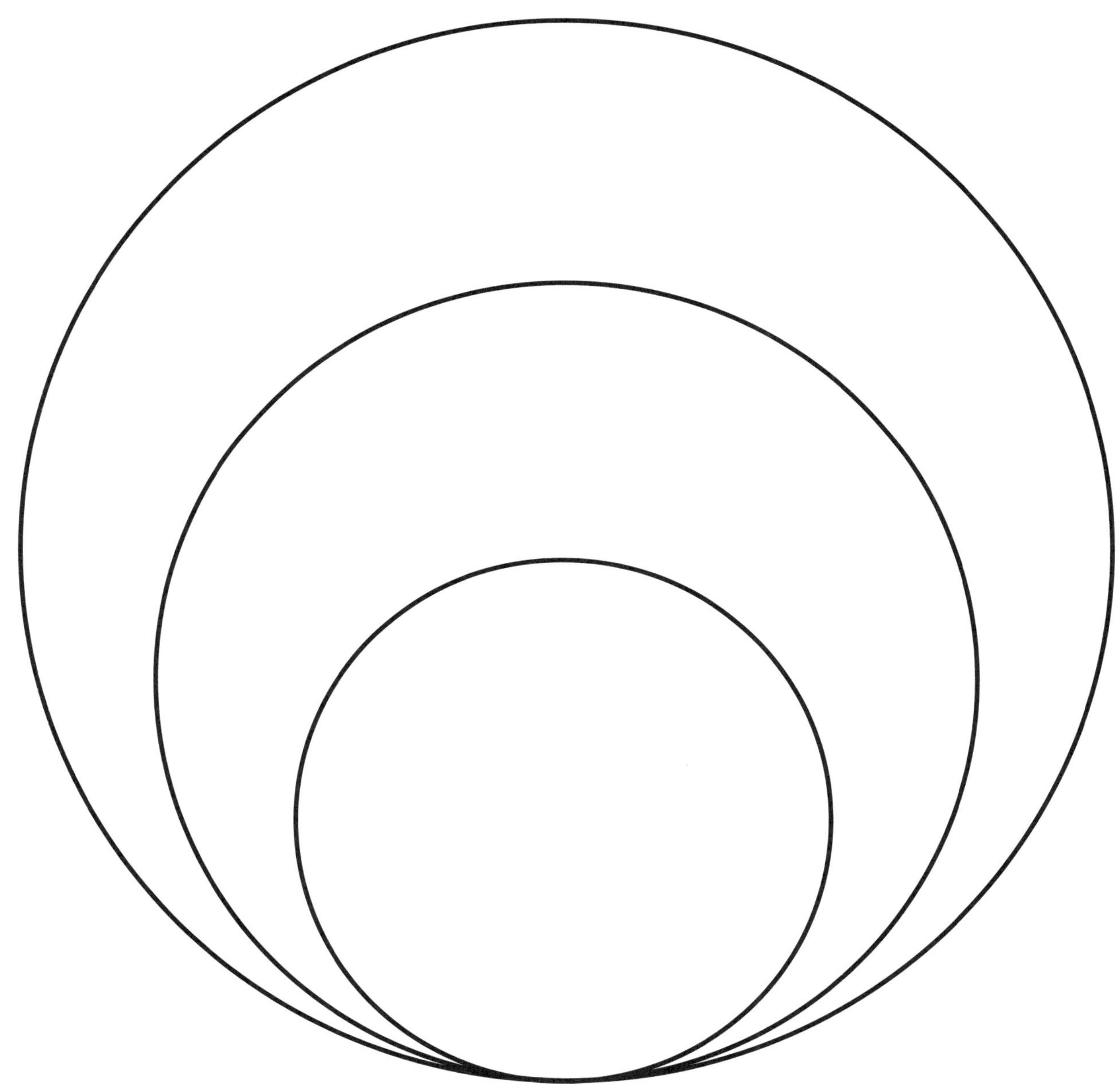

HOW YA DOIN? ☐ ☐ ☐

Author: Priscilla Shumway

Description: To better adjust your training session to meet the specific needs of the learner, it is important to understand what they already know and are comfortable with and what they may be struggling with. This activity helps to direct the learning session to meet the learner's perceived needs.

Objective: To have the learner identify areas of strengths and weaknesses for the process or skills covered in that day's session

Audience: Hands on skills training, such as participants who work on a manufacturing line

Time: 10 minutes

Group Size: One-on-one or one-to-few

Materials: List of the daily skills

Process: Present the learner with a list of the specific skills, processes, or piece of machinery that you expect to cover that day. Show her the piece of equipment or physical skill you will be teaching that day. Ask her which skill she can perform most competently and which skill she is least competent in.

Begin with that in which she is most competent in order to start out on a positive topic. Check her understanding and clarify any misunderstandings that may occur. Move on to the next step in the process or skill, building on her knowledge base. At the end of that day's session, ask her to now rate her knowledge or skill on those areas covered. Ask her to plan out what she wants to cover during the next session.

Debrief: Ask if she has had prior experience on the process or skill in another job. How are they similar? What did she do at another job that will help her with this new knowledge or skill?

Variations: It may be necessary to perform the skill first so that the participant can gauge whether or not she knows how to perform the skill or process. If the participant has done other similar tasks, this will help her see how the tasks differ and where she may need reinforcement.

NAME THAT TERM! ☐ ☐ ☐

Author: Karen Carlson

Description: The trainer and participant toss around a soccer ball labeled with training content jargon that needs to be defined.

Objective: To familiarize new employees with commonly used terms and acronyms. This activity helps a new employee understand the terms and acronyms commonly used in the workplace. This could be used as a pre- and post-training assessment as well.

Audience: New employees or employees transferring from one department to another

Time: 5–7 minutes

Group Size: One-on-one or one-to-few

Materials: Soccer ball, marker, list of terms and acronyms and their definitions

Process: Prior to class, write commonly used terms and acronyms on the spots of a soccer ball. Toss the ball gently to your participant. Ask the participant to read the term or acronym closest to his right thumb and attempt to define the term or acronym. Assist him as needed to reinforce the learning.

Debrief: Clarify any terms or acronyms that remain unclear. Provide the participant with a list of terms and acronyms along with their definitions.

Variations: Prior to class, write numbers on the spots of the soccer ball. Have your list of terms and acronyms numbered to match the numbers on the ball. Toss the ball gently to a participant, who shares the number nearest his or her right thumb. Then read the term/acronym or definition for the participant to answer. This variation allows you to use the soccer ball for multiple topics or classes.

☐ ☐ ☐ SET UP FOR SUCCESS CHECKLIST

Author: Priscilla Shumway

Description: This checklist helps the trainer set up the training room prior to the session to ensure the participant has the necessary materials, can see and hear the session, and has access to the right equipment.

Objective: To complete a set-up checklist prior to a hands-on training session, helping to ensure the success of the training

Audience: Appropriate for audiences participating in hands-on training such as with machinery, with equipment, or in a lab

Time: 5 minutes

Group Size: One-on-one or one-to-few

Materials: Checklist

Process: Prior to working with learners in a facility where they must work on machinery, complete the checklist on the following page. You may customize it for your environment.

Debrief: None

Variations: This checklist should be customized to each training environment. For example, if you are training in a computer lab, what software documentation would you need? Is there a log-in ID needed? What are the Wi-Fi requirements? Is there on-line help?

Set Up for Success

Assemble training documentation: one per learner	
Lay out tools	
Lay out job aids: one per learner	
Check equipment to ensure it is working	
Prepare chart of topics to be covered	
Set up area: Can learners see everything? Can they hear the instructor and A/V? Is the area clean?	
Check safety equipment and provide personal protective equipment (PPE) if necessary	
Provide proper clean up materials	
Provide reasons to learn: what is the importance of doing the job correctly?	
Determine the entry level/basic skills needed to do the job.	
Other: • Raw materials • Supplies • Gauges • Fixtures • Security systems • Emergency equipment • Software systems • Information processing equipment • Reports and logs	

TRAINER POSITIONING FOR ONE-ON-ONE

Author: Rich Meiss

Description: Trainers often struggle with how to position themselves when training one-on-one or one-to-few. Here are some time-tested strategies that have worked for many participants in our Bob Pike Group one-on-one training classes.

Objective: To help trainers determine how to position themselves when training one-on-one or one-to-few

Audience: One-on-one or one-to-few

Time: No extra time needed

Group Size: Usually fewer than six people

Materials: Classroom table, regular chairs, bar stool

Process: Set up the training class so that you, the trainer, can assume one of three positions:

1. Standing in front of the participant. When you are in "teaching mode," assume this position in the front as you would in leading any training session. In this role, you are giving instruction, perhaps with some PowerPoint slides or other visual aids.

2. Seated on a bar stool in front of the participant. Use this position when leading a question-and-answer session, when holding an informal discussion, or when wanting to assume a more relaxed posture with the participant.

3. Seated at the table with the participant. Use this position when you want to indicate that you are at a "peer level" with the participant. In a sense, you become his or her learning partner. This is also a good way to allow the participant to become the instructor, leading a "teachback" session for you and any other participants. (See the exercise in the Revisiters section called "Teachback for One-on-One Training.")

Debrief: None

WORKPLACE GPS

Author: Karen Carlson

Description: This exercise provides participants with a visual of where to find people and places in the workplace.

Objective: To assist employees in locating the people, tools, and places they will need on the job

Audience: New employees or employees transferring from one location to another

Time: 5–7 minutes; longer if doing an actual walking tour

Group Size: One-on-one or one-to-few

Materials: Map blueprint of the floor(s) or buildings the employee will be using, highlighter or pen

Process: Using the map, show the participant where she will find the location of: her work station, key coworkers, restrooms, break areas, supply or copy rooms, etc. Ask her to write in important information or highlight key areas.

Debrief: Expand on the information or answer questions as appropriate. Encourage the participant to keep the map as a job aid.

Variations: Once the map is complete, go on a walking tour of the area covered. Introduce the employee to fellow coworkers and other key contacts.

SCORE FOR ONE-ON-ONE TRAINING—SUPER CLOSERS, OPENERS, REVISITERS AND ENERGIZERS

REVISITERS

Interval reinforcement is one of the best gifts you can give your students and one of the best ways to maximize content retention. In his research, Albert Mehrabian determined that a person exposed to an idea six times over the course of a month would retain greater than 90 percent of the information learned after one month. Expose your learners to content one time? Mehrabian found retention is less than 10 percent after 30 days. This is why we suggest revisiting content six times in different ways over the course of your class and using follow-up techniques after.

Unfortunately, most learning events today cover ideas one time and expect the participants to remember them. Maybe the reason this happens is that trainers believe it is boring to repeat themselves over and over. But doing a revisit doesn't have to be boring. Creative trainers find interesting ways to allow the participants to do the revisit, thus making it more interesting and effective. So here's the key: review is when the trainer does it, and revisit is when the participants do it. Therein lies the power—getting the participants to revisit.

Here are some tips for helping participants retain more from your sessions:

- Revisit early and often. Remember, we need to cover key content at least six times for maximum retention.
- Don't call it "review." In our sessions, we suggest trainers avoid the "R" word (review) and instead use the word "revisit." The difference is that the instructor is the one who usually does a review, covering the content again, while in a revisit, the participants are going over the content another time in a more interesting way.
- Use a variety of revisiting techniques. This keeps the interest level of participants high and helps them stay engaged in the learning process.

The following pages contain some of our favorite revisiting techniques for one-on-one training. Each is very powerful. Enjoy learning and employing these techniques, knowing that ultimately your learners will be the ones to benefit!

DO-IT-YOURSELF JOB AID

Author: Adrianne Roggenbuck

Description: The participant will fill in a job aid in stages throughout the training. After each segment of training, he will revisit that part of the process and record it on his job aid. When the training is over, he will have a completed job aid to refer to back on the job. This will help him to recall the steps in the process he has learned.

Objective: To revisit each step of the process being taught and complete a job aid

Audience: Participants in any training that teaches steps in a process

Time: 5 minutes after each segment of content

Group Size: One-on-one or one-to-few

Materials: Job Aid template (may be copied onto cardstock)

Process:

1. After completing the first segment of content for step one in the process you are teaching, introduce the job aid template showing all steps in the process. Explain that the participant will be filling in the form as he learns each new step until he has completed all the steps. Then he will have a cheat-sheet or job aid that he can use to implement the new process back on the job.

2. After each segment of content, allow 5 minutes for the participant to fill in that step with the details of how to complete that step and any tips he can add to ensure success.

3. At the end of the training, the participant will have a completed job aid to take with him for use back on the job.

Debrief: This job aid can be used anytime you need to remind yourself of one or more of the steps in this process.

Variations: Template may be customized by adding rows or columns. Depending on how many steps there are in the process, the job aid may be more than one page long. It is recommended that it does not exceed one page on both sides.

Job Aid Template	
Steps in Process	**Tips**
1.	
2.	
3.	
4.	
5.	
6.	

Permission granted by the authors to duplicate this page.

5 WS AND 1 H

Author: Scott Enebo

Description: This activity is designed to move beyond the day-to-day activities of a trainee and to see how everything is connected including who is involved, what needs to be included, when things need to happen, where certain things take place, why we are doing it and how it needs to happen.

Objective: To generate questions on your content that connect what participants are learning with the bigger realities of the work being done

Audience: Any training audience

Time: 10–15 minutes

Group Size: Any size, including one-on-one or one-to-few

Materials: 10-20 index cards per person

Process:

1. Say, "In just a moment, you and I are going to take 5 minutes and write questions on index cards for each other based on the content that we have covered. The only trick is that each question must start with one of the following words: Who, What, When, Where, Why or How. For example:
   - Who is involved in...?
   - What are the key components to...?
   - When should you take action on...?
   - Where could you find...?
   - Why would we...?
   - How can I...?"
2. Allow time for you and your participant to write questions on index cards.
3. Collect both sets of cards and shuffle them together. Distribute all of the cards to you and the participant in equal numbers.
4. Take turns asking each other the questions posed. Ask a specific person (if more than two) and have that person respond. Fill in any incomplete or incorrect information as answers are given.
5. Continue as long as time allows.

Debrief: This activity does not require a debrief as it is positioned as a content revisit.

Variations:

1. Save these cards and use them for future trainees as a way to get them to explore and recall content covered.
2. Use the cards to create a quiz or test on the content.

HOW TWEET IT IS! ☐ ☐ ☐

Author: Priscilla Shumway

Description: The learner distills key content into 140 characters as if it were a tweet on Twitter.

Objective: To evaluate and apply the most important content in a recent lecture or session. Having to distill the most important content into 140 characters forces the learner to focus on the "need to know" information and how she will use the content.

Audience: Any training audience

Time: 5–7 minutes

Group Size: One-on-one or one-to-few

Materials: Index cards or an actual Twitter account

Process: Ask the learner to consider sending a tweet that explains the most important concept she learned during the lecture or training session. It must be no more than 140 characters. If she has a Twitter account and a phone or computer with her, she can post it. If she does not have any of the above, have her write it out on index cards. She can then share her insights with the instructor or any other participants.

Debrief: Ask her to explain why she chose this concept and how she will use this information on the job.

Variations:

1. What is a Facebook posting she might write about the training?
2. Take a photo that she could post on a social networking site that lets others know about the training.

I CAN DO THAT

Author: Scott Enebo

Description: While each of us can describe and reiterate information that we are taught, can we do it backward? How about without words? With our eyes closed? Put your skills to the test as you try and revisit content in new and creative ways.

Objective: To follow instructions on selected cards to revisit key content

Audience: Experienced learners

Time: 5–15 minutes

Group Size: One-on-one or one-to-few

Materials: Cards created for "I Can Do That" (see next page) in the appropriate stack; tub of Play-Doh

Process:

1. Copy and cut out the cards from the template on the next page. Then make three stacks of cards with the 1s in one pile, the 2s in their own pile, and the 3s in their pile.
2. On the blank "2" cards, the trainer should write a series of processes or tasks that the learner should be able to act out or work with. For example, "the sales process," "stages of the customer service plan," or "primary safety concerns." These will then create a task for the learner based on information from cards in stacks 1, 2 and 3. For example, the learner will:

Stack 1	Stack 2	Stack 3
Demonstrate the	Stages of the customer service plan	In order
Write on paper the	Primary safety concerns	With your eyes closed

3. Say, "We are going to take turns and draw a card from each of the piles here: 1, 2 and 3. According to what we draw, we will then act out the idea presented in the way prescribed." *Note: It may be that the cards drawn don't exactly meet the topic covered. In that case, simply draw an additional card to bridge the gap.*

Debrief:

- What content was most familiar for you?
- What topic was most unfamiliar for you?
- What is something that you think you would like to look at in greater depth?
- What steps will you take to get more familiar with that topic?

Variations: Add different cards to the deck that better meet your needs. Be creative and have fun with what you are teaching to better drive engagement and retention!

Stack 1 – Task	Stack 2 – Process	Stack 3 – How
Draw the		Behind your back
Explain the		In order
Demonstrate the		Backward
Advocate for the		Without words
Write on paper the		With your eyes closed
Restate the		Through pictures
Describe the		Left handed
Represent the		Right handed
Interpret the		Using props
Diagram the		Using sound effects
Share a story of the		With PlayDoh
Critique the		Without jargon

☐ ☐ ☐ LETTER LIST

Author: Scott Enebo

Description: Do you ever wonder what your brain is storing? Roll the die and see what comes out! Take whatever letter is rolled and come up with as many ideas about the content that you can that start with that letter. As you compete with one another, you only get points for unique answers that the other person did not think of.

Objective: To encourage learners to recall and extract key learning ideas for the session or day

Audience: Any training audience

Time: 5–15 minutes

Group Size: 2–10 people

Materials: 26-sided die with a letter of the alphabet on each side (available on Amazon), or letters of the alphabet written on pieces of paper

Process:

1. Roll the 26-sided die and see what letter comes up.
2. Using the letter that comes up, each person will then come up with words, concepts, phrases or ideas about the topic of the training that start with that letter and write them on a piece of paper. Allow 2 minutes for them to think of as many ideas as possible. The trainer participates if the session is one-on-one.
3. Set the timer and begin.
4. After time expires, have your learner share his list. If you have other learners, they then shout out if they have the idea that was shared. If this is the case, then the reader does not get any points. A point is awarded to players for each unique answer given.
5. After the first person shares, other learners can share if they are present. Otherwise, the instructor shares while the participant looks for unique answers and ideas.

Debrief: If you are using this as an opener, ask:

- What is one concept that you know a lot about?
- What is one that you would like to know more about?

Allow learners time to mix and mingle as they share information that they know and learn about the items that they did not know as much about. If the participant is alone, have him share with you as you converse back and forth.

If you are using this as a closer, ask:

- Based on what we have talked about, what is one thing for which you have a new appreciation for or understanding?
- What are you going to start doing based on that realization?

If you are using this as a revisit, ask:

- What did you find easy/difficult to recall or use?
- Where do you need to spend a bit more time?

Variations: Allow a person to roll the die twice and then select the letter that he likes best.

LIVING GLOSSARY ☐ ☐ ☐

Author: Marc Ratcliffe

Description: Rather than having a static glossary in the back of the book that no one reads, "Living Glossary" provides an ongoing reinforcement tool and enables revisiting of key terms covered in the training.

Objective: To identify the meaning of acronyms, ambiguous terms and otherwise difficult words used during the training

Audience: Any training audience

Time: On-going

Group Size: One-on-one or one-to-few

Materials: Pens and sufficient paper (or access to word processing options)

Process:

1. At the beginning of the training, introduce the concept of the "Living Glossary." Explain that during the session, there may be unfamiliar terms, jargon or acronyms used by the instructor or contained in the course materials. Assure your participant that it is appropriate to clarify these "on the run"' using the Living Glossary section of the books/ e-resources.

2. When an ambiguous term is identified by a participant, the trainer should direct her to the Living Glossary section of her resources and provide a suitable definition. Have her record the definition for future reference. As time permits, the trainer could provide an official definition and then ask the participant to restructure the term into her own words. This will promote additional reinforcement of the term or concept.

Debrief: Although debriefing is happening on an on-going basis, the trainer could revisit the Living Glossary at the end of the day to extend further understanding. Additionally, the trainer could collect all the new glossary entries and create a quiz where the participant needs to match terms with their correct definitions. This could easily be done face-to-face or online.

Variations: As an extension, the trainer could challenge the participant to catch the trainer using unexplained terms or jargon for which she would win a reward (candy, points for her team, dots for a prize auction or similar). When challenged, the trainer should then provide a definition on the spot and have the participant transcribe this in her Living Glossary.

NEW HIRE HUMAN SCAVENGER HUNT

Author: Priscilla Shumway

Description: It is often helpful for a new hire to become familiar with the company by talking to a variety of other employees. By preparing a human scavenger hunt, it allows the employee a chance to discover more about the company and other jobs within the organization.

Objective: To familiarize the employee with the inner workings of the company such as other jobs, employees, functions, mission, vision, human resource programs

Audience: New hires

Time: 1–2 hours depending on the size of the company

Group Size: One-on-one or one-to-few

Materials: List of people to visit and questions to answer

Process:

1. Create a list of possible people that the new hire should visit and interview questions he might want to ask in order to learn more about the company and his new job function. Work with the participant to explain each of the departments and have him brainstorm and write down questions he wants to have answered.

2. Then give him a time limit, and send him out to interview the appropriate people/departments and get his questions answered. Be sure to schedule this with the other employees and departments so that the new hire can find the people he needs to speak with at the appropriate time.

3. Have him return to the training room and be prepared to share what he has learned.

   Examples of departments to visit and questions to ask:

   - Employee who is currently doing the same job as the new hire: What is the most important piece of advice you can give me starting out? What is an aspect of the job that most people would not believe that you do?

   - Employee who used to do that job but was promoted: What skills did you need to move up from this position? What skills served you best when you did this job?

   - Direct supervisor: What qualities do you look for in a good employee? What are some factors that will help me be most successful in this job?

     Marketing
     Human Resources
     Research and Development
     Sales
     Warehouse
     Facilities Management

Debrief: After he has shared his results with you, ask him what additional questions this scavenger hunt may have raised for him about his new job and the company.

Variations: If you have a small group of learners, you can assign them different people to meet and different questions to ask. They then report back to the whole group.

QUIZ IT 

Author: Adrianne Roggenbuck

Description: The participant will write several questions after each segment of content that capture the key ideas. At the end of the training, she will take the quiz she has created.

Objective: To revisit the key concepts throughout the training and complete an assessment at the end of the training

Audience: Any training audience

Time: 5 minutes following each segment of training to write the questions and 10 minutes at the end of the training to take the quiz

Group Size: One-on-one or one-to-few

Materials: Index cards (three per person for each segment of content)

Process:

1. After the first segment of content, give the participant three index cards. Have her revisit the key concepts from the previous segment and write two or three quiz questions about them. Have her write the question on the front of the index card and the answer on the back. Each question should be written on a separate index card. Tell her she should approach this as though she was writing a quiz for another participant to take to ensure his mastery of the content.

2. Repeat the process after each new segment of the training. The questions should zero in on critically important ideas or information.

3. At the end of the training, select 10–12 of the index cards with key concepts that you feel are important for the participant to remember, and give her her own quiz. Read each question out loud and either have the participant answer orally or in writing.

4. Give her the index cards she wrote to check her answers.

Debrief: Have the participant keep the index cards as reminders of the key concepts.

Variations:

1. If you have more than one participant, they can actually give their quizzes to another person.

2. Have participants type their quiz questions with spaces for the answers to create a quiz in an electronic format which can then also be printed.

ROOTS AND BRANCHES

Author: Scott Enebo

Description: As a botanist might tell you, trunk, branches, leaves and roots all play a vital role in the growth and development of a tree. While the leaves and branches are what we see and appreciate, it is only because of the roots that this is possible. With every topic we cover, there are "roots" that support our processes and give the basis for what we do, while the implementation or "branches" is what we can see on a daily basis. This activity helps to create a visual of learning covered, put it into context, and action plan how it might be implemented back on the job.

Objective: To create a visual of core foundations that were learned and how those supportive practices or skills can be applied on the job

Audience: Any training audience

Time: 5–10 minutes

Group Size: One-on-one or one-to-few

Materials: Chart paper and markers

Process:

1. Hang a piece of chart paper on the wall with a simple tree trunk drawn in the middle.
2. Say, "We are going to take some time to put everything that we have learned into context. We are going to use the image of a tree to help us describe and differentiate between types of ideas and material covered. On this paper, we are going to draw some roots, and we are also going to add some branches and leaves.

   "Each root that is added will represent a core model, technique or support that is in place that helps us do our work. Each branch added to the tree will represent how to implement and use information, as well as tips and techniques that will make it easier to do our work. As with roots and branches, there are always offshoots, so if you need to add sub items for the larger branches or roots, feel free to do so."
3. Do an example of a root and branch together to show what good might look like. For example, if teaching machine safety, a root might be the company safety procedure for a given machine. A branch would be the practical steps and ideas that could be implemented to ensure safety on the job, including specific practices.
4. Allow 5–10 minutes to add to and create more roots and branches. As the facilitator, you may choose to serve as a co-participant to help add ideas and keep things moving. Consider giving this tree some color to add depth and dimension and make it more memorable.

Debrief:

- As you look at this tree, what is one root that you find most critical to your success?
- What is one branch that you have added that will make your work easier when implemented?
- What is something that you would ensure every person taking this training would better understand and take back to the job?

Variations: Before beginning the root and branch creation, ask the learner what type of tree best represents the work being discussed in the training and then use that image as you draw representative roots and branches. For example:

- Evergreen—Working in a service industry, you need to be ready to help regardless of circumstances. We need to be like the evergreen and consistent no matter what is going on.
- Oak—Being an industry leader, you need to be long-lasting and strong. Customers count on us to be there for them for years to come.
- Weeping willow—Get creative here!

STORYBOARD

Author: Marc Ratcliffe

Description: A storyboard is a series of visual panels, like a comic strip, which includes rough sketches outlining the sequence of actions. Commonly used in film scripts, this activity uses a storyboard to bring words and pictures together to provide an engaging means of promoting reinforcement of key content.

Objective: To create a storyboard to reinforce key content or a series of steps

Audience: Any training audience

Time: 20–25 minutes

Group Size: One-on-one or one-to-few

Materials: Pens and paper (or equivalent e-tools)

Process:

1. Provide each participant with a copy of the Storyboard template (see the following page).
2. Describe what a storyboard is and explain that your learner is going to create a storyboard based on a topic covered during the session.
3. The trainer should model how to complete the storyboard template and highlight the four key sections of the storyboard:
   - Image Box—where the learner provides a sketch of what is happening in each shot
   - Action—this explains in words what is happening in the picture
   - Dialogue—this is the narration that supports the visuals in the image box. It is like the voice-over heard in a film
   - FX—this involves any music or sound effects that could be included to add meaning to the images and dialogue
4. Finally, the participant should be encouraged to create her own storyboards based on content from the session. Where necessary, the trainer may suggest a list of suitable topics from which to choose.

Debrief: Once the storyboards are completed, the participant should present her final products to the trainer and her peers. The trainer should provide feedback and seek additional clarification if needed. This activity enables the trainer to ascertain the level of knowledge retained.

Variations:

1. As an extension, the participants could create their work in an e-format and publish it on their blogs, wiki or other shared learning space.
2. Participants could also be encouraged to produce a short video of the storyboard via their smart phones or similar tool and upload it to a video sharing site or organizational learning platform.
3. This activity could be used as part of a revisiting activity or at the beginning of the next session as a revisiting tool and a link to new content.

Storyboard Template

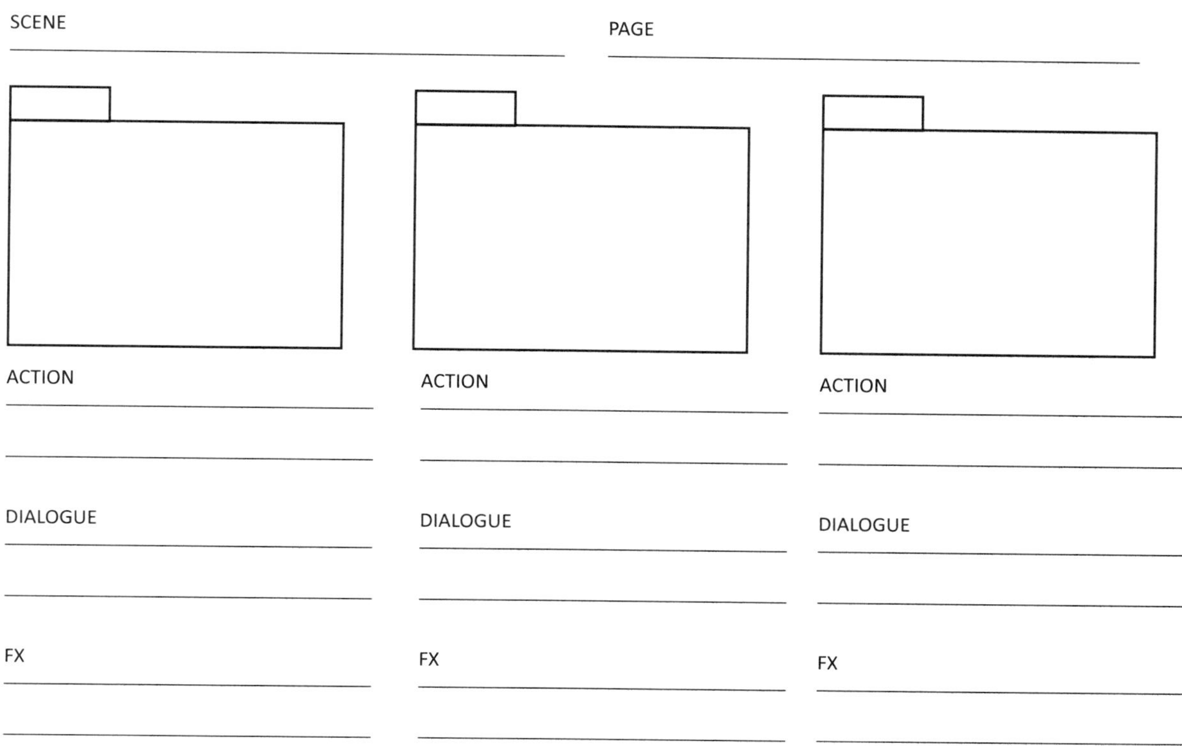

Storyboard Example – Manual Handling

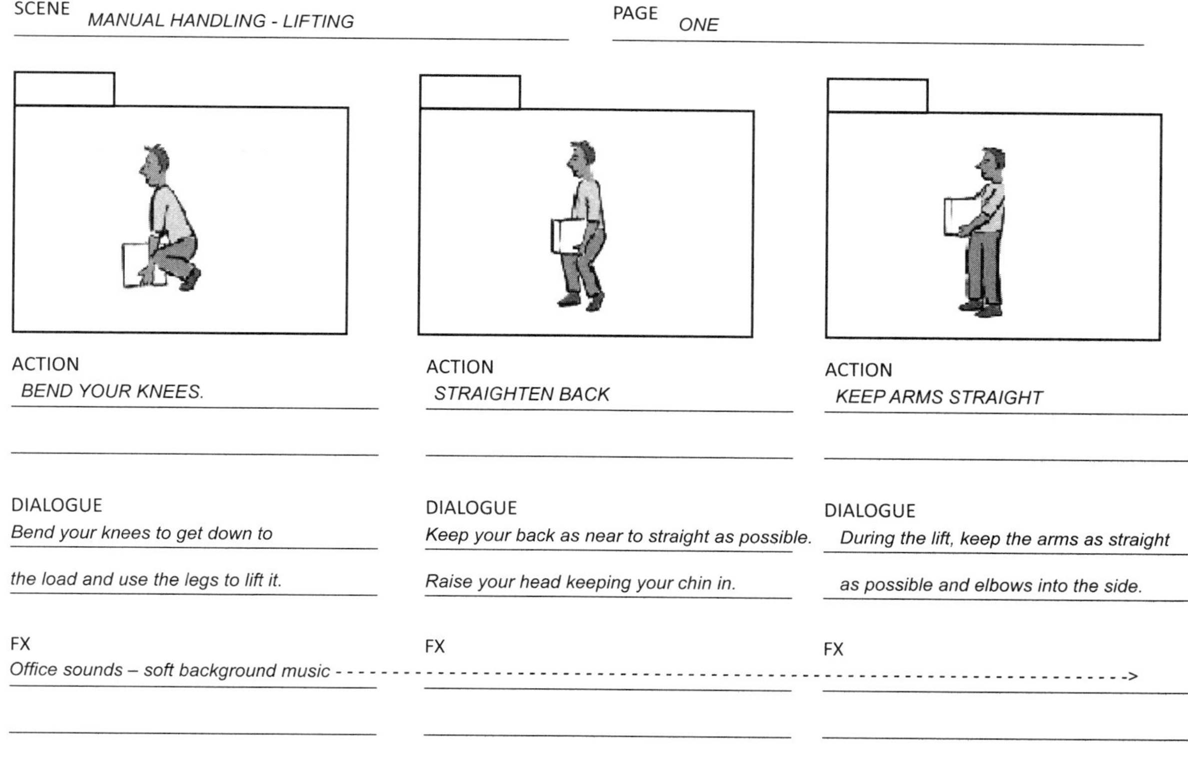

Permission granted by the authors to duplicate this page.

TEACHBACK FOR ONE-ON-ONE TRAINING ☐ ☐ ☐

Author: Rich Meiss

Description: The participant acts as the instructor and either re-teaches content already visited or researches and presents new information.

Objective: To have the participant learn more by teaching or revisiting material

Audience: Any training audience

Time: 15 minutes or more, depending on the objective

Group Size: Any size audience, including one-on-one or one-to-few

Materials: Good teaching materials such as a text, article, reference book, etc.

Process:

1. Assign each participant in a small group a chapter or section of the reference book. Give participants a certain time period (usually 10 to 15 minutes) to scan through their assigned sections, highlighting or noting the key points from that section. In one-on-one training, you may assign an entire section, chapter or learning piece to the participant, and ask him to train you as if you didn't know the content.

2. After the study time is up, give each participant 2–3 minutes to share three to five points from his or her assigned section. Encourage the other group participants to follow along, marking the pages or highlighting the information in that section that is valuable to them. You, the instructor, should join in the learning group as a participant when teaching one-on-one or one-to-few. Continue the process around the group until all have shared. In one-on-one training, you may allow the participant more time to do the teaching piece.

3. If appropriate, have a question and answer session on the content covered, or give the participant a few moments to reflect on what he has learned and add any key ideas to an action idea list.

Debrief: Spend any appropriate time clarifying what was covered.

Variations: Encourage participants to "teach" the information in a creative way. They may do a skit, create a visual presentation of the information, put the key content into an advertisement, or find some other creative way to present it. *Note: This variation will typically require more preparation time, but it is more fun and engaging.*

VERBAL TENNIS ☐ ☐ ☐

Author: Scott Enebo

Description: Imagine watching a tennis match. Someone serves and then a rally ensues. Back and forth the ball goes, waiting for one person to make a mistake. Translate this idea to your class. One person serves up an idea, and you then have to add to it. The server then adds to it again until someone gets stumped and a point is won! If the server loses, the opponent then gets to select a topic and the game continues.

Objective: To encourage recall of key ideas, processes or concepts in order to bring them back to active memory and then apply and use them on the job

Audience: Any training audience

Time: 5–10 minutes

Group Size: One-on-one or one-to-few

Materials: Piece of paper

Process:

1. Say, "We are about to play a game of Verbal Tennis. What this means is that one of us will throw out a topic, and the other person will need to come up with an idea that relates or builds on it. The person who started the conversation will then add even more, thus returning the idea back to the other person. This continues until someone gets stuck and can no longer add ideas. Whoever gets that last idea will win a point. We will play to 5 points." (Feel free to decide how long you play or how often.)

2. "Take the next 3 minutes and look through your materials. As you look, decide what topics you think we should discuss and perhaps some things that you know more about."

3. "After 3 minutes, we will flip a coin to see who will go first and then throw out the first topic and start to keep score!"

Debrief: This is a revisit technique and can simply be used to revisit and engage throughout. If you wish to debrief this activity, here are some questions that you might consider:

1. What content was most familiar for you?
2. What topic was most unfamiliar for you?
3. What is something that you think you would like to look at in greater depth?
4. What steps will you take to get more familiar with that topic?

Variations:

1. When doing one-on-few training, consider making this a "doubles match" and have people play in pairs. Each team can then keep score as you build teamwork.

2. Incorporate a time limit for tasks that need to have rapid response times so that the participant has to have learning readily available.

WALKING THE TALK ☐ ☐ ☐

Author: Priscilla Shumway

Description: When training people on machinery, it is important to know they can translate what they have learned in the classroom back to the shop floor. This activity reinforces classroom theory with practical application on the shop floor.

Objective: To provide the learner with the opportunity to label and explain the parts of a process or manufacturing line

Audience: Participants from a manufacturing facility or those in any hands-on training environment

Time: Varies based on the complexity of the process or equipment, but it should not last more than 1 hour

Group Size: One-on-one or one-to-few

Materials: Any equipment in a lab, manufacturing plant, machine shop, etc.

Process:

1. After teaching the basics in the classroom on the process and/or machinery that the learner will be using, bring the learner into the lab or shop floor.
2. Have her name each piece of the manufacturing line, equipment or machinery and explain what it is used for. Then have her explain the process and how each piece of equipment is used in the process.
3. Once she has mastered that, begin to ask her questions such as:
   - Why do you have to do step A before step B?
   - What would happen if....?
   - When would it be necessary to...?

Debrief: People often learn a skill through muscle memory and do not actually understand the process involved. Therefore, when something goes wrong, they are unsure of how to correct the problem. It is important to understand the theory (classroom) and be able to articulate it in practice (on the floor).

Variations: If you have several participants in the training program, you can assign pairs to take one piece of equipment or a process and walk everyone through that process or part of the line.

WHAT'S A GOAL TO DO? ☐ ☐ ☐

Author: Doug McCallum

Description: The trainer and participant discuss the purposes and rewards of goal-setting and then together make a list of goals to complete for the year along with graphics to represent those goals.

Objective: To make a visual goal board because "what the human mind can see and believe, it can achieve"

Audience: Any training audience focused on accomplishing goals or tasks

Time: 10–90 minutes

Group Size: One-on-one or one-to-few

Materials: One 18"x24" poster board, magazines with pictures that can be cut out, one glue stick and scissor per person

Process:

1. Instruct the participant to think about some realistic goals to achieve and some "out there" goals that could be achieved with a little effort.
2. Ask the participant what his plan of attack will be to reach those goals.
3. Tell him to think big and shoot for the moon because even if he misses, he will land among the stars!
4. Have him look through as many magazines as possible looking for pictures that will represent one of the goals.
5. Now have him cut out the picture and paste it on the poster board in whatever creative manner he wishes.
6. Ask him to present his poster to you, the instructor, with a full explanation of what the poster board means to him and why.
7. The poster board should be placed where the participant can see it on a daily basis.
8. In one year, do a debrief and see how many goals were met or exceeded. Give a reward of some kind for those goals that were achieved.

Debrief: When you are attempting to set goals, understand that visualization is important in attaining those goals. Do some research on visualization and cite examples of those that have used visualization to meet their goals.

Variations: This activity could also be applied to larger groups, but it works better with fewer participants around a table of magazines networking and getting ideas from each other. Accountability is important in this exercise. Drawing pictures will work but not as well as cutting out pictures.

SCORE FOR ONE-ON-ONE TRAINING—SUPER CLOSERS, OPENERS, REVISITERS AND ENERGIZERS

ENERGIZERS

MENTAL STIMULATORS and PHYSICAL ACTIVATORS

Great presentations and training sessions keep participants energized through the use of effective presentation methods as well as mental stimulators and physical energizers. And if you're training one-on-one, keeping the energy up in the room is no less important than if you had a crowd!

This section of the SCORE book offers a variety of energizers to keep your participant active and engaged. Energizers are useful throughout a session and probably are most useful during these times: after lunch, after a break, when the room temperature is too warm, and during the middle of a long content presentation.

Make sure to use these types of activities purposefully and strategically. Your learner should have a sense of why you are doing them. Using simple statements such as "Okay, let's get our minds focused back on the learning process by starting with this simple quiz," or "Let's wake up our brains this afternoon by examining this trivia test" will help your participant understand why you are doing the activity or exercise. And, while energizers are not required to tie into the content, many of these activities do, so if you are looking for more revisiting ideas or openers, don't forget to look through here, too!

This section contains both mental stimulators and physical energizers. The mental stimulators create "mental sparks" that stimulate the brain and keep a participant ready to learn. This set of activities includes trivia tests, storytelling, and activities that are larger than life! Mental stimulators are useful after breaks or after lunch as a way to re-focus the learner on the topic at hand or to stimulate the brain and get a participant back into a learning mood.

When used correctly, mental stimulators literally create energy in the group. You can see the physical energy increase through the mental stimulation. The activities included here are easy to use. Copy them and hand them out to your participant or read them to the learner at appropriate times.

Physical activators get the body moving. These activities are often simple, competitive and fun. They range from things like simple breathing exercises to kinesthetics. Some of these physical activators are also designed to be controlled stretch breaks. That is, they involve some questions or activities that can be related to the session content, thus creating a double win—a stretch for the participant and a learning point to be communicated.

When used correctly, physical activators will get a participant back into a learning mood with a refreshed body and a re-focused mind. Although many of these are not content-related, most participants will make the connection between the activity and the purpose for which it was intended—to help the learning process. Enjoy these new energizers!

ANCHOR IT ☐ ☐ ☐

Author: Janice Horne

Description: The learner re-enacts a time when he felt empowered and confident.

Objective: To equip a participant with a physical action to invoke a feeling of confidence or empowerment

Audience: Those who are learning a new skill and may be uncomfortable with it

Time: 5 minutes

Group Size: One-on-one or one-to-few

Materials: None

Process:

1. Ask your participant to stand up.
2. Invite him to recall a time when he felt really good and confident about something he had accomplished. Then invite him to mimic his physical state when he felt empowered.
3. Then instruct him to throw down an imaginary circle on the floor in front of him with his hand. Now have him recall that confident time again and, when you say "Go," he is to step into the circle in front of him in his empowered state. [Typically the learner will be standing up straight with his shoulders back, his head erect, a smile on the face, etc.]

Debrief: Ask your learner how that feels. Then inform him that, before he begins practicing his new skills, simply adopting the confident posture and stepping into the imaginary circle in front of him will help him actually become more confident.

Variations: Have the learner create physical anchors for key learnings he wants to remember.

BLAST-OFF BREAK ☐ ☐ ☐

Author: Adrianne Roggenbuck

Description: When your participant needs a quick physical break to re-energize, have her do a blast-off break. She will stand, count, and then spring up in the air to blast off. This quick energizer will get her blood flowing and help her "reach for the stars."

Objective: To re-energize participants after they've been sitting for a period of time

Audience: Any training audience

Group Size: Any size audience, including one-on-one or one-to-few

Time: 2 minutes

Materials: None

Process:

1. Ask the participant to stand up and make sure she has some space around her to move. Tell her that she is going to experience a blast-off break.
2. Tell her to count down from 10 to zero as though she were counting down to a rocket launch. As she is counting, she will bend her knees further and further until she is crouching and can place her hands on the floor by the time she gets to zero.
3. Then have her spring up and reach for the stars as she says, "Blast off!"
4. You may repeat the activity two to three times in succession to increase the level of energy.

Debrief: When we want to "reach for the stars," we have to learn the steps to success before we launch ourselves into space. Let's now continue to learn those steps with renewed energy.

Variations:

1. This could be used as a quick opener for a short training session. You would debrief by telling your learner that, in today's session, she will be learning the steps she needs to take in order to prepare herself to "reach for the stars."
2. You could have your participant "reach for the stars" periodically throughout the session and then, as a closer, she would list the steps to success that she learned before she blasts off one final time.

FACE OFF 

Author: Becky Pluth

Description: The instructor and learner take turns reading questions or statements on a card and then replying in this fast-paced format that can combine content revisiting and networking.

Objective: To get the energy up in the room while revisiting content

Audience: Any

Time: 2–5 minutes

Group Size: One-on-one or one-to-few

Materials: Cards with pre-written statements

Process:

1. First, determine the purpose of your face-off. For example, this exercise could be used to practice building a skill like interviewing, discuss a text, or role play. These tasks and assignments should be written down on cards with one task or question per card. Some content ideas for the cards might include:

   A. A short text which then asks how you should respond to the information

   B. A teaching assignment ("Teach me the login protocol.")

   C. Skill practice ("Role play giving feedback on a job poorly done.")

   D. An opinion survey ("What are your thoughts on...?")

   E. Test questions ("What does the ADDIE model stand for?")

   F. Or a fun fact ("Share something about yourself.")

2. Instruct the learner to sit face-to-face with you.

3. Distribute a stack of the cards to both you and your learner.

4. Begin by reading what is on your card, and your learner will attempt to quickly respond with the correct answer.

5. After one card is answered, the learner will share what is on her card.

6. Continue going back and forth for whatever length of time. This exercise can be repeated several times throughout the day as a way to get the energy up, learn about one another and revisit content.

Debrief: Share with the learner the correct responses to questions that were missed or off slightly.

Variations: This activity could also be adapted to larger groups but done in table groups.

GIVE IT A MINUTE ☐ ☐ ☐

Author: Becky Pluth

Description: A variety of quick exercises to allow the learner to stretch and get energized

Objective: To get the energy up in the room. It gets both you and your learner out of the sitting position and gets his body engaged. This could be a mental break after a quiz or just after a longer section of content. These can be done for fun but could also be modified around content for an academic challenge.

Audience: Any

Time: 1–5 minutes

Group Size: One-on-one or one-to-few

Materials: Depending on the exercise, you may need one sheet of paper per person or a can of soda.

Process:

1. Steady Eddie. Stand and exhale completely. Then inhale through the nose for 6 seconds and out through the mouth for 6 seconds. Repeat a couple of times.

2. Fake Laugh. In your mind, imagine the most ridiculous thing you can think of and, on the count of three, start laughing as hard as you can. Get the offices next door wondering what is going on in there.

3. Wiggle Jiggle. Some of us jiggle while others just wiggle. Stand up and get all of those knots out with a good vigorous wiggle. Start with hands and then add shoulders, hips, legs, feet and head. Go crazy and make any noise you want.

4. Race down the hall, but don't get caught. Race, skip, hop to the restroom, but if anyone happens along, you must walk as though nothing was happening until he or she is out of sight, and then commence the activity again.

5. Soda Slam. Pour fizzy soda in a shot glass and see who can complete the slam first without snorting.

6. Paper Airplanes. Each person (including the trainer) has 1 minute to create. Winner takes all...whatever "all" is.

7. Earlobe Massage. Using your pointer finger and thumb, massage each lobe simultaneously. Apply pressure and pull down, massaging gently, and draw focus to the forefront of your mind.

8. Temple Massage. Pointer and index fingers to massage both temples simultaneously. Apply pressure gently and draw focus to the forefront of your mind.

Debrief: Ask how your learner felt before versus after. Ask yourself how you feel!

Variations: None

LEARNING WALK ☐ ☐ ☐

Author: Rich Meiss

Description: Take the participant on a walk—around the shop/office/plant or just around the training room, and use the time to point out various aspects of what has been learned and clarify additional information. Additionally, trainees may be introduced to other employees who've been contacted beforehand and asked to share some knowledge they have about the topic.

Objective: To create some energy for the trainer and participant while teaching new ideas and/or reinforcing content already taught

Audience: Any training audience

Time: 10–30 minutes

Group Size: One-on-one or one-to-few

Materials: None

Process:

1. Tell the participant that you are going to go on a Learning Walk. Explain that during this walk, you are going to be doing one or several of the following:
   - Revisiting key concepts taught in the class by viewing some of the posters and other visuals displayed in the training room
   - Discovering some new ideas by talking to other employees
   - Viewing an area where: products are made, customers are served, processes are being completed, etc.
2. Go on the Learning Walk and take whatever time is needed to complete the objective.

Debrief: Although most of the learning happens in the process of the walk, you may get reactions and answer questions once you return to the training room.

Variations: None

MAKE A WORD ☐ ☐ ☐

Author: Marc Ratcliffe

Description: "Make a Word" is a mental energizer that has a participant create a list of words using a finite selection of letters. There is also a message he has to untangle using all of the letters.

Objective: To focus the participant on the session and sharpen his cognitive skills. Doing brain stimulating activities that involve variety and complexity can help build the cognitive reserve of participants and set them up for success in their learning.

Audience: Any training audience

Time: 5 minutes

Group Size: One-on-one or one-to-few

Materials: Pens and paper

Process:

1. Provide the participant with the following letters either on the board or on a handout:

M C E E R R O O S

2. Explain that he will have 3 minutes to create a list of words of 3 letters or more using only the letters above. Unlike similar word games, there are no restrictions on the type of words that could be listed. As such, nouns and plurals are acceptable.
3. At the end of the 3 minutes, ask the participant to tally up his list.
4. Advise him that 5–10 is good, 11–15 is very good and 16 or more is excellent.
5. If there is more than one participant, award prizes for the participant with the longest list of qualifying words.

   Words could include: core, corer, crème, err, moo, more, moor, moors, mere, morose, ore, room, rose, Rome, some, sore, score
6. Finally, provide the participant with an additional minute to see if he can find the hidden message in the letters. There are two words, one of four letters and one of five letters. (Answer = MORE SCORE, or SCORE MORE)

Debrief: Explain that this was a useful brain warm-up designed to build up his cognitive reserve for the day. Also, it is important to highlight the importance of structure and reorganization. For example, the letters lacked meaning individually; however, when combined and reorganized, many meaningful solutions were created. Furthermore, this thinking could be applied to a variety of training and business situations.

Variations: Rather than using MORE SCORE or SCORE MORE for the make-up of the letters, the trainer could use a message that is more relevant to her subject matter. This activity could then be turned into an opener, as the hidden message then becomes a focusing device for the session.

THE MYTH OF MULTI-TASKING

Author: Rich Meiss

Description: The learner writes the numbers 1–26 and then the letters A–Z before repeating the process in a different way to highlight the inefficiency of trying to multi-task.

Objective: To encourage learners to put away distractions in the training room (including e-toys) so that they gain the maximum benefit from the training.

Audience: Any training audience

Time: 5–7 minutes

Group Size: Any size audience, including one-on-one or one-to-few

Materials: Paper and pen for each participant, stopwatch, flip chart paper and marker

Process: When you have a participant who is distracted and not giving her full attention to the training, suggest that you'd really like for her to get the full benefit of the class. Explain that while most people believe they can multi-task, recent research reveals that we don't multi-task, we alternate-task. Ask her to take part in an activity that will confirm this fact.

1. Say, "In a moment, I'd like to ask you to take a piece of paper and a pen, and get ready to do a timed activity. When I say 'go', I will start my stopwatch, and I'd like you to write numbers 1, 2, 3, 4, and so on up through number 26 on the top part of your paper from left to right. Then, underneath the numbers, write the letters of the alphabet, A–Z. Again, you'll be writing all 26 numbers, 1-26 on the top of the paper from left to right, and then all the letters of the alphabet, letters A–Z, under the numbers. As soon as you have finished your task, please stand up. What may I clarify?"
2. Say "Go," and start your stopwatch. On a chart pad or piece of paper, record the time at which the participant stood. If there are additional learners, record the first person standing, when the majority of the group stands, and when the last person stands. Thank the group, and tell them to be seated. (It will usually take most people between 30-50 seconds to complete this task.)
3. "Now, we are going to repeat the process, but this time I'd like you to write the number 1 on the top line, and then directly under that write the letter A. Then write number 2, and underneath that write the letter B, until you have again written all 26 numbers and all 26 letters. And again, please stand when you are finished. What may I clarify? Ready, go!" Again, write down the time the participant finishes.

   [The process looks like this:]

   1 2 3 4 5 6 7 8 9 10 11 12 13 14 15 16 17 18 19 20 21 22 23 24 25 26

   A B C D E F G H I J K L M N O P Q R S T U V W X Y Z

Note: I have never had anyone finish the second exercise more quickly than the first, and often the times are significantly longer the second time.

Debrief: Ask the participant why the second writing exercise took longer than the first one. Then discuss the challenge the brain has in juggling two different things at the same time (mixing the writing of the numbers and letters versus just concentrating on one or the other). Explain that this is the same process at work when you attempt to multi-task in the classroom or in any other situation. Encourage participants to give their full attention to what they are learning.

Variations: None

NAME THAT ACRONYM

Author: Adrianne Roggenbuck

Description: The participant will write down the meanings of 5–7 acronyms.

Objective: To energize the participant by using humor and creativity

Audience: Any training audience in an organization that uses acronyms

Time: 5 minutes

Group Size: One-on-one or one-to-few

Materials: List of 5–7 acronyms on a handout, chart paper, or PowerPoint slide

Process:

1. Give the participant the list of 5–7 acronyms. Tell him that he will have 2½ minutes to write them out. He should be familiar with some of them, but some of them might be unfamiliar.

2. The goal is to spell all of them out within the time given even if he has to make something up. The only wrong answer is no answer.

3. At the end of the given time, have him share his answers with you. You can then reveal the correct answers to the pertinent acronyms and some fun ones you made up for the others.

Debrief: Acronyms only have meaning to us if we agree on what they stand for. For today, let's agree on how we will use these acronyms going forward.

Variations:

1. This activity could also be used as either a revisit of acronyms your participant has learned so far during the training, or an introduction to new acronyms he is expected to know.

2. Another variation would be to instruct the learner to create his own acronym(s) related to the content or process being learned.

Sample Acronyms

Select 5–7 of these, or use your own.

BASIC	Beginners All-purpose Symbolic Instruction Code
BDU	Brain Dead User
CASH	Computer Assisted Self-Help
COBOL	Common Business Oriented Language
HTTP	Hypertext Transfer Protocol
IPTV	Internet Protocol Television
MEGO	My Eyes Glazed Over
PICNIC	Problem In Chair Not In Computer
PLOKTA	Press Lots of Keys to Abort
SMOP	Simple Matter of Programming

POWERBALL ☐ ☐ ☐

Author: Becky Pluth

Description: The participant, in a race against time, works to correctly identify steps in a process or parts of a product.

Objective: To identify what the learner already knows about a concept so you can spend more time coaching the areas that are fuzzy or in which the learner lacks confidence. If it takes longer than 12 seconds for certain labels to be placed, a coach or instructor can assume the learner is guessing and can then spend more time on that concept or content. This will also get the energy up at the beginning of the session by working with a physical product or walking to the wall.

Audience: Any

Time: 5–10 minutes

Group Size: One-on-one or one-to-few

Materials: A deck of cards you've created with the steps of a process or parts of a product, one envelope, timer, chime, one product or poster of the process for the participant to label

Process:

1. Instruct the participant that, in just a minute, he will take out the contents of the envelope, select one, and then place that card at the correct spot on the product (or poster).
2. Explain that he must grab only one card then race up to the product, place the card where he thinks it belongs and then run back to the envelope. A timer will be running until each card is placed and he rings the chime to show he's done.
3. Once all of the cards are placed, he can choose to take a minute to rearrange.
4. Start the timer as he begins. Stop the timer once the chime has been rung.
5. Move right into an interactive lecturette by walking through all of the cards and arranging/rearranging as needed.
6. Have the learner take notes and share why he placed the cards where he did, when it makes sense.
7. As a close before break, mix up the cards and have your learner repeat the exercise. Point out the time differential between the two as well as how his accuracy changed from the first attempt to the second.

Debrief: No debrief is necessary as it has already been done throughout the exercise.

Variations:

1. This activity could also be done privately as a paper–pencil assessment instead of at the wall and with a timer.
2. As a revisit, the learner could create cards himself by just looking at the product or the model.

SOFTWARE SCROUNGE ☐ ☐ ☐

Author: Karen Carlson

Description: This hunt helps participants locate key web sites, files and applications commonly used throughout the company.

Objective: To familiarize participants with where they will find relevant information on the computer that they need to do their job

Audience: Any training audience, especially new employees

Time: 10 minutes

Group Size: One-on-one or one-to-few. If it is one-to-few, it is best done in pairs.

Materials: List of clues for items to locate on the computer

Process:

1. Develop a list of approximately 10 pieces of information the employee will need to access on the computer on a regular basis.
2. Create clues to lead the employee in the right direction. Is it on the network? In the customer relationship management software? On the company website? Is there somewhere else the employee should know to look for information like an employee wiki? Tell the participant to locate as many of the items as she can in the amount of time provided.
3. Optional: Encourage her to take screenshots or copy the URL for each item she locates.

Debrief: After the hunt, ask the participant if any of the items were hard to find. Then show her how to find any items she was unable to locate.

Variations: This could also be done as a revisiter if the content has already been covered in class.

THAT'S NEWS TO ME

Author: Adrianne Roggenbuck

Description: This mental energizer gets the participant thinking about the top 10 newspapers still in print as of 2012. He will list the top 10 and compare to the actual list taken from *Top Ten of Everything 2012* by Caroline Ash.

Objective: To re-energize the participant by using a mental energizer unrelated to training content

Audience: Any training audience

Time: 5 minutes

Group Size: One-on-one or one-to-few

Materials: Paper for participant, chart or PowerPoint slide with top 10 list, timer, prizes

Process:

1. Ask the participant to think about the top 10 daily newspapers that were still in print as of 2012. Tell him he will be writing down as many of those top 10 as he can think of in the next 2 minutes.
2. Give the participant a piece of paper to record his answers and start the timer.
3. After two minutes, call time. Reveal the top 10 newspapers starting from number 10 and working back to number 1.
4. The participant will award himself one point for each newspaper he has correctly listed. If he has listed the newspaper in the correct ranking, he receives two points for that newspaper (one for the correct newspaper, one for the correct ranking).
5. Have the participant add up his numbers and write down his total.
6. Prizes may be awarded for different point levels.

Debrief: None

Variations:

1. Use the top 10 Sunday papers in the U.S. instead of daily newspapers.
2. This could be tied to a revisiter later in the day. Have the participant think about the key concepts he has learned in the session and pretend that he is a reporter for one of those top 10 newspapers. Then have him write an informative article which highlights those key concepts.

Top 10 Daily Newspapers in the U.S.	Top 10 Sunday Newspapers in the U.S.
1. *The Wall Street Journal*	1. *The New York Times*
2. *USA TODAY*	2. *Los Angeles Times*
3. *The New York Times*	3. *The Washington Post*
4. *Los Angeles Times*	4. *Chicago Tribune*
5. *The Washington Post*	5. *Daily News (New York)*
6. *Daily News (New York)*	6. *San Jose Mercury News*
7. *New York Post*	7. *Houston Chronicle*
8. *San Jose Mercury News*	8. *The Philadelphia Inquirer*
9. *Chicago Tribune*	9. *Detroit Free Press*
10. *Detroit Free Press*	10. *The Arizona Republic*

Sample Prize Point Categories

Prize Level 1	0-3 points
Prize Level 2	4-8 points
Prize Level 3	9-14 points
Prize Level 4	15-20 points

TO JUGGLE OR NOT TO JUGGLE — THAT IS THE QUESTION

☐ ☐ ☐

Author: Doug McCallum

Description: The participant will attempt to juggle several balloons at one time. He will then describe what it felt like as balloons were added to the challenge and as they dropped to the ground.

Objective: To help the participant understand that there is a limit to the number of tasks one can juggle at one time or the number of action ideas he can implement from the training

Audience: Any training audience

Time: 5–10 minutes

Group Size: One-on-one or one-to-few

Materials: 5–7 medium-sized balloons

Process:

1. Instruct the participant to blow up 5-7 balloons as fully as possible.
2. Now have him write action ideas he wants to implement from the training on the balloons with a felt tip marker.
3. Let him start by juggling one balloon, which should be pretty easy. Continue to add balloons, and he will find that the juggling becomes more difficult.
4. Continue the process to make the point that it is impossible to successfully juggle all of the balloons at one time.

Debrief: Have a conversation about task management and how many action ideas the participant can effectively put into action from the training. Encourage him to pick the 3-4 highest value ideas and begin to implement them first. He can then add additional action items over time.

Variations: Have the participant break the balloons after they fall and ask how it feels. Does it relieve the feeling of attempting to juggle too much? Or exacerbate a feeling of failure?

☐ ☐ ☐ # WHAT IS THIS?

Author: Scott Enebo

Description: This is a mental stimulator designed to wake up the brain and allow fresh ideas to come out. Each person takes everyday objects from around the room and asks the other person "What is this?" The other person is allowed to answer with any response other than the actual name or function of the object. What will *your* brain come up with?

Objective: To ignite the brain to think of new and creative ideas needed to reimagine current obstacles

Audience: Any training audience

Time: 3–5 minutes

Group Size: One-on-one or one-to-few

Materials: Random items from around the room

Process:

1. Say, "I am going to select an object from this room and I am going to ask you 'What is this?' You are then going to respond in any way that you see fit, but you cannot say the actual name of the item or its normal function. For example, I might show you a pencil and say, 'What is this?' You cannot say it is a pencil or a writing implement, but you might say 'It's a miniature telephone pole,' or 'It's a javelin for Smurfs.' Be as creative as you like. After you have made a guess, you then get to choose an item from the room, and I will tell you what it is in the same fashion."

   Here are a few ideas to start your idea generation:

   - Paper Clip—Leg trap for cockroaches or new age ice skates
   - Power Cable—Top secret National Security Agency listening device or a lion tamer's whip
   - Sticky Note Pad—Eye patches for aspiring pirates or do-it-yourself playing card deck creation kit
   - Stapler—Alligator in disguise or miniature can crusher

2. Alternate as many times as desired in order to wake up the mind.

Debrief: None

Variations:

1. Instead of alternating items, select one item in the room and then take turns deciding what it is. When no new ideas are apparent, move on to a new item and see what ideas surface. For example, select a coffee mug. Ideas that might come out:
   - Miniature hot tub
   - Extreme skateboard park
   - Village water well
   - Black hole
   - A very hungry mouth
   - Trash can for gum wrappers

2. Turn this into a competition. When one person selects an item, all participants give an answer of what the item could be. Continue in the same order as learners try and add new ideas to the same topic. When one of the participants cannot answer, she or he gets a point. The person with the fewest points at the end of play is the winner!

WHAT'S YOUR POINT?

Author: Adrianne Roggenbuck

Description: This is a physical energizer that also revisits content. The participant will stand up to answer questions by pointing to the ceiling, floor, or wall.

Objective: To energize participants physically and to challenge them mentally

Audience: Any training audience

Time: 5 minutes or less

Group Size: One-on-one or one-to-few

Materials: A list of multiple choice or true/false questions that may revisit content

Process:

1. Prior to the training, create a short list of 5–7 multiple choice or true/false questions. These may include questions based on your content.
2. When the participant is exhibiting signs of fatigue or brain overload, have her stand up and stretch out her arms to get warmed up for a quick quiz.
3. Tell her that you will be asking her a short series of multiple choice or true/false questions. If it is a multiple choice question and the answer is A, the learner should point to the ceiling. If the answer is B, point to the wall. If the answer is C, point to the floor. If you are asking true/false questions, then "true" is the ceiling and "false" is the floor.
4. Ask a question, give the answer choices and then say, "What's your point?" The participant will point to the ceiling, wall or floor to select her answer.
5. When she gets an answer correct, have her "raise the roof" by pressing both palms up to the ceiling several times.
6. Continue until you have asked all of the questions on your list. The participant should now be re-energized.

Debrief: None

Variations:

1. The questions could be theme-related or about the company instead of content-related.
2. Random questions could also be used. See the sample questions.

Sample Questions unrelated to training content:

1. The largest turkey raised in the U.S. weighed:

   A. 33 pounds

   B. 23.5 pounds

   C. 26 pounds*

2. Which country has the longest reigning living monarch?

   A. United Kingdom

   B. Thailand (Bhumibol Adulyadej: 68 2/3 years as of January 2015)*

   C. Denmark

3. Which U.S. state produces the most potatoes?

   A. New York*

   B. Idaho

   C. Missouri

4. Which of these artists has the most platinum albums in the U.S.?

   A. Garth Brooks*

   B. Elvis Presley

   C. Michael Jackson

5. Which of these is the top film franchise of all time?

   A. Star Wars

   B. James Bond

   C. Harry Potter*

** Denotes correct answer.*

ABOUT THE AUTHORS

Becky Pike Pluth, M.Ed., CSP, MPCT
With more than 15 years as a training professional and two training industry best-selling books on the market, Becky Pike Pluth, The Bob Pike Group's president and CEO, doesn't rest on her laurels. As proof of her desire to continuously strive for "great," Becky was named one of *Training* magazine's Top 40 under 40 in 2012. She is the author of the award-winning *101 Movie Clips that Teach and Train* and *Webinars with WoW Factor*.

Rich Meiss, MBA, MPCT
Rich has been a participant-centered trainer with The Bob Pike Group and other leading train-the-trainer organizations for more than 25 years. He has designed and taught numerous workshops to more than 65,000 trainers and leaders worldwide. His personal approach causes audiences to warm to him instantly. Most of his work is with repeat clients who continue to ask specifically for him. Rich is author or co-author of nine books including *Coaching for Results* and *SCORE! 1–5 Super Closers, Openers, Revisiters, Energizers*.

Karen Carlson, MPCT
With more than 15 years of experience in learning and development, Karen has a proven track record of exceeding customer expectations and catering delivery and materials to the unique needs of each client. She includes adult learning methodology and recognizes the diverse learning styles of her audiences when designing materials.

Scott Enebo, M.A., MPCT
Scott Enebo is a strong advocate and model for creative and interactive training as he continues to see the impact it has on the participants experiencing the learning. Scott received his master's degree in intercultural relations with a focus on multicultural training. He also is trained in the ICA's Technology of Participation and enjoys conducting participatory strategic planning and action planning sessions.

Janice Horne, MPCT
Janice has a drive and enthusiasm for training and is motivated by the end result—an improved training experience by those who learn from her participants. Having thrived in retail, financial, and government organizations, Janice brings a wealth of skills to adult learning to help businesses focus on results-based action. Janice also is author of *The ABCs for Happy Living*.

Doug McCallum, M.Ed., MPCT
Doug McCallum has been training adults for more than 45 years and is recognized as one of the top national and international training professionals by his peers. He has conducted workshops and trainings for over 62,000 professional teachers, trainers and corporate leaders and given more than 150 keynote addresses. Doug has authored or co-authored four other books.

Marc Ratcliffe, M.Ed., MPCT

Marc founded MRWED Training and Assessment in Brisbane, Australia in 2000, which quickly became one of Australia's leading providers of trainer training. It has received numerous awards including the 2010 LearnX award for Best Workplace Trainer Training Program. Marc was recently named Queensland/Northern Territory Learning and Development Person of the Year for 2013 by the Australia Institute of Learning and Development. He is the author of *The Trainer's Toolkit* and *The Trainer's Cook Book*.

Adrianne Roggenbuck, M.Ed., MPCT

Since joining The Bob Pike Group, Adrianne has championed Research-based Creative Teaching Strategies and Designing Lessons that SCORE, two workshops specifically for teachers. As a dynamic, memorable and inspirational trainer, Adrianne presents regularly at education conferences. She also is an adjunct instructor for graduate-level classes at Aurora University and Waubonsee Community College in Aurora, Ill.

Priscilla Shumway, M.Ed., MPCT

As a senior trainer for The Bob Pike Group, Priscilla brings a wealth of experience in adult education and technical training to her sessions and is a two-time recipient of the Pike's Peak Performer Award for content and facilitator performance. Priscilla has advanced studies in Accelerated Learning, Integrative Learning and Learning Styles. She also was a contributing author to *The Experts' Guide to the K-12 School Market* and is co-editor of *Real Women, Real Leaders*.

OTHER BOOKS BY THESE AUTHORS

101 Movie Clips that Teach and Train

Using short clips from movies can relay learning points more dramatically and quickly than any lecture.

Let this award-winning book jumpstart your creativity for lesson planning or training design by providing you with the perfect movie clip for over 100 topics including discrimination, leadership, team building, and sales.

Each clip comes with cueing times, plot summary and scene context, and cogent discussion questions. All topics are cross-referenced so you can easily find the perfect clip for your teaching or training needs.

SCORE! series

The SCORE! series of books is a compilation of activities that will help engage your learners while ensuring your content is remembered long after class is over.

These activities for Closing your session with impact, Opening your session with relevance, Revisiting content creatively, and Energizing your learners will make you a learning legend and improve training retention.

Books in this series include general CORE activities as well as a focus on technical training, webinar training and one-on-one training.

Books in this series:

SCORE! Volume 3

SCORE! for Technical Training, Volume 4

SCORE! for Webinar Training, Volume 5

Webinars with WoW Factor

Death by webinar is rapidly replacing death by PowerPoint! But it doesn't have to. Make webinars effective and engaging.

Teaching online is a different animal—requiring different skills and a different energy—that completely exposes any weaknesses in your material and preparation. In this book, Becky Pike Pluth shows trainers where to start when moving to an online platform and what pitfalls to avoid along with explaining some of the basic webinar tools trainers can use to make online training interactive. Becky includes 40 activities that will help even a novice webinar trainer create an online training that has impact and builds in long-term retention.

All these titles and more great resources for training effectively are available from The Bob Pike Group at www.BobPikeGroup.com/shop-products or by calling (952) 829-2658 or (800)-383-9210.